At Issue

| Does the Internet
| Increase Anxiety?

Other Books in the At Issue Series

At Issue

Does the Internet Increase Anxiety?

Tamara Thompson, Book Editor

GREENHAVEN PRESS
A part of Gale, Cengage Learning

GALE
CENGAGE Learning·

Farmington Hills, Mich • San Francisco • New York • Waterville, Maine
Meriden, Conn • Mason, Ohio • Chicago

GALE
CENGAGE Learning™

Judy Galens, *Manager, Frontlist Acquisitions*

© 2016 Greenhaven Press, a part of Gale, Cengage Learning.

Gale and Greenhaven Press are registered trademarks used herein under license.

For more information, contact:
Greenhaven Press
27500 Drake Rd.
Farmington Hills, MI 48331-3535
Or you can visit our Internet site at gale.cengage.com

Articles in Greenhaven Press anthologies are often edited for length to meet page require-ments. In addition, original titles of these works are changed to clearly present the main thesis and to explicitly indicate the author's opinion. Every effort is made to ensure that Greenhaven Press accurately reflects the original intent of the authors. Every effort has been made to trace the owners of copyrighted material.

Cover photograph reproduced by permission of Brand X Pictures.

LIBRARY OF CONGRESS CATALOGING-IN-PUBLICATION DATA

Does the Internet increase anxiety? / Tamara Thompson, Book Editor.
        pages cm. -- (At issue)
    Includes bibliographical references and index.
    ISBN 978-0-7377-7382-8 (hardcover) -- ISBN 978-0-7377-7383-5 (pbk.)
    1. Internet--Psychological aspects. 2. Information technology--Psychological aspects. 3. Anxiety. I. Thompson, Tamara, editor.
    HM851.D626 2016
    303.48'33--dc23
                                    2015029476

Printed in Mexico
1 2 3 4 5 6 7 20 19 18 17 16

Contents

Introduction

When transcendentalist author Henry David Thoreau wrote in *Walden* that "men have become the tools of their tools," he was talking about the negative effects that the Industrial Revolution's technological advances were having on American society in 1854. But he just as easily could have been commenting on our modern society's current obsession with mobile devices.

Visit any public place and it quickly becomes apparent just how deeply involved Americans have become with the mobile technology of smartphones, tablets, and other devices that allow users to access the Internet anywhere and at any time. On public transportation, in restaurants and movie theaters, on street corners, and even in the middle of crosswalks, it can sometimes seem like every single person has their head down, tapping at a device, and their near-constant public use has become the punch line for countless late-night jokes and scathing social commentaries.

Mobile devices, of course, serve a wide array of important functions that have become integral to users' lives; they facilitate everything from banking and bill paying to getting driving directions, occupying cranky toddlers in the back seat of cars, finding a restaurant or a ride, and keeping on top of the news and up to date with friends and family on social media.

According to the 2015 "Internet Trends" report by the consulting firm Kleiner, Perkins, Caufield, Byers, more than half the US population uses a smartphone to access the Internet, and 2015 daily consumption of digital media was nearly 5.6 hours per person—51 percent of it on mobile phones. For young people, social media is the primary reason for Internet and smartphone use; in spring 2015, 74 percent of American teens used Facebook, 59 percent used Instagram, 57 percent used Snapchat, and 32 percent used Twitter, according to the "Internet Trends" study.

Nearly 90 percent of Millennials (individuals born from the early 1980s to early 2000s, roughly those aged fifteen to thirty-five) reported that "my smartphone never leaves my side, night or day,"[1] and 80 percent said that checking their phone is the first thing they do when they wake up, even before brushing their teeth.

The demand for mobile devices isn't likely to slow anytime soon. According to the web-based statistics portal Statista, US smartphone use is expected to grow from 182.6 million in 2015 to more than 220 million by 2018. Globally, the number is expected to reach 5 billion by 2017, with China and India being the biggest adopters of the technology.

But as much as smartphones, tablets, and computers are useful tools to keep users connected, informed, and entertained, they are also shaping the behavior of their users, and not always for the better—just as Thoreau observed that the telegraph and steam engine were doing in his own time. Many experts say that the constant connectivity of today's mobile devices is eroding social skills and having a detrimental effect on mental health. As the authors in this volume's viewpoints discuss, the Internet has the potential to increase anxiety in a variety of ways:

- The constant connectivity of smartphones can be so addictive that many users experience the anxiety of "nomophobia"—palpable stress and discomfort from being disconnected or out of touch—when they are prevented from using their devices.

- Multitasking with various forms of technology—such as texting while surfing the web or talking on the

---

1. Mary Meeker, "Internet Trends 2015," Kleiner, Perkins, Caufield, Byers, May 27, 2015. https://kpcbweb2.s3.amazonaws.com/files/90/Internet_Trends_2015.pdf?1432738078.

phone while gaming or watching streaming video—has been linked to both depression and anxiety.

- On social media, the fear of missing out (FOMO) can worsen existing social anxiety disorders and can also create new anxieties about real-life interactions.

- Searching for health information online can increase anxiety because even when people search for common and innocuous symptoms, 70 percent of the time the results show information about serious and rare conditions instead.

- Cyberbullying in chat rooms or by text, e-mail, social media, or any other digital means can have serious consequences, including anxiety, depression, and suicidal behavior.

- The more hours spent gaming online, the stronger the link to social anxiety disorder, social phobia, depression, and even pain.

- Being constantly exposed to information coming from multiple sources can cause a digital information overload that makes people feel stressed, anxious, and out of control of their lives.

- Activity-tracking devices that are linked to the Internet provide minute details of the "quantified self" but can lead to hyper-vigilance and anxiety about weight, exercise, and body image.

In his recent book, *iDisorder: Understanding Our Obsession with Technology and Overcoming Its Hold on Us*, research psychologist Larry Rosen makes the case that using digital technology the way most people do means that consumers, by and large, exhibit a wide variety of symptoms that are typically associated with serious mental health diagnoses—including antisocial personality disorder, social phobia, anxiety disorders, autism, obsessive-compulsive disorder, attention-deficit hyper-activity disorder, narcissistic personality disorder, hypochon-dria, body dysmorphia, voyeurism, schizotypal and schizoaf-fective disorders, and addiction—a troubling constellation of symptoms he has dubbed "iDisorder."

"We are being compelled," writes Rosen, "to use technolo-gies that are so user friendly that the very use fosters our ob-sessions, dependence, and stress reactions."[2] Rosen goes on to say, however, that the solution is not to give up technology al-together. "That's not possible," he writes, "we are way too past the point of no return. But it is not too late to recognize the craziness that technology *can* promote and discover new ways to stay sane in a world that encourages—and even promotes—insanity."[3] The key, says Rosen and other experts, is modera-tion, and indeed millions of people are still able to interact with their mobile devices in a healthy way.

As Rosen concludes, "Paying attention is half the battle. Watch how you interact behind the screen. Pay attention to the words you use, the pictures you post, and the interactions you have with people. Pay attention to websites you visit and technologies that you use to see if they might be causing symptoms of an iDisorder. . . . It's all about being aware and monitoring your behavior around all of these marvelous tech-nological inventions."[4]

Because, as Thoreau observed so long ago, humans should be the masters of their tools, not the other way around.

The authors in *At Issue: Does the Internet Increase Anxiety?* present a wide array of viewpoints that explore the various positive and negative impacts of Internet technologies and consider the ways in which digital technology consumption can be both healthy and harmful.

2. Larry Rosen, *iDisorder: Understanding Our Obsession with Technology and Overcoming Its Hold on Us.* New York: Palgrave Macmillan, 2011, p. 4.
3. Ibid.
4. Ibid.

1

Mobile Device Separation Anxiety Is a Growing Problem

Olivia Rahim

Olivia Rahim is editor-in-chief of Social, *a lifestyle magazine.*

The ubiquitous use of smartphones in modern society has created a new psychological malady: nomophobia, the anxiety or fear experienced when one is unable to access technology. Losing a smartphone or being unable to get online can make a nomophobe very stressed and uncomfortable, and that itself can be a symptom of an addiction to technology. Experts suggest limiting the time spent on mobile devices and paying deliberate attention to in-person relationships and activities so one's digital life does not become more important than what is happening in the real world.

Everyday technology consumes everyone's lives as the phone, computer, tablet and other high tech devices have become not just an object, but also a close companion. And for those who are extremely connected to their devices, going without them, even for only a few minutes, can be an anxiety-filled experience.

A majority of American adults (56 percent) own smartphones, according to a recent study by the Pew Research Center. Having the ability to check your mail, play games and browse the Internet right in your pocket is a leap forward for technology and staying connected to the workplace, but it may come at a cost.

Nomophobia, or the pathological fear of remaining out of touch with technology, is a relatively modern affliction. It's basically a side effect from changes the mobile phone has made to human habits, behaviors and even the way we perceive reality. Entire relationships are becoming defined through mobile texting and colorful little emoticons, from saying "I love you" to "I think we should move on."

Nomophobia is a result of people becoming more and more electronically connected to the point that their technology-based network and relationships become their home community.

So how did it come to this? Have smartphones become an extension of Americans or is everyone simply becoming victims of a fast-paced, always connected society? Chances are it's a little bit of both.

Dr. Chuck Howard, licensed psychologist and chair of the psychology programs at Argosy University, Denver, believes it can be more complex than simply stamping a label on the problem.

"Electronic Banishment"

"Nomophobia is a result of people becoming more and more electronically connected to the point that their technology-based network and relationships become their home community," says Howard. "Losing that connection is essentially a form of electronic banishment. They fear being tossed out of, or losing their 'social village.'"

The term was originally coined from a 2010 study by You-Gov, a UK-based research organization that wanted to look at anxieties suffered by mobile phone users. The study found that men and women often felt stressed when their mobile phones were turned off.

"Nomophobia can be a symptom of a potential addiction," says Howard. "Users who are happy and having a good time when on their device, then face great stress and anxiety without it. They may obsess about it. They can't put it down. This is when actual addiction becomes a threat."

When you see a behavior becoming destructive, and admit to having a problem, you can handle it in the same way as other types of addiction. "Develop strategies for meeting your social needs in other ways . . . without depending on an electronic platform," suggests Howard.

Coping Strategies

Start by resisting the urge to constantly check your phone. Try limiting your number of mobile social media networks and consider joining more in-person professional networking groups or sports clubs. Set aside some time to leave your phone alone, such as at dinner, with friends or going to sleep.

If it becomes an addiction and begins to strain your relationships, consider asking others around you what they think. Be open to a sort of intervention where friends and family may candidly tell you their thoughts.

No need to go cold-turkey, just take some small steps at a time to disconnect and enjoy the world around you, without looking through a smartphone screen. And lastly if you can't do it alone, then seek professional help.

2

"Nomophobia" Is an Artificially Created Disorder

Mario Lehenbauer-Baum

Mario Lehenbauer-Baum is a clinical and health psychologist as well as a certified industrial/organizational psychologist. He is also a passionate gamer who uses new technologies frequently.

The idea that the discomfort caused by losing one's smartphone is somehow a psychological condition that is linked to both addiction and phobia is absurd. The behaviors associated with so-called nomophobia do not meet the diagnostic criteria for addictions, nor do they have anything to do with a phobia, as it is properly defined. In an era when so much personal information and social connectedness is dependent on a smartphone, it is natural to feel discomfort if it were to be lost, but it is not a mental disorder. Nomophobia is an artificially created condition.

The term "nomophobia" describes the fear of spending time without your phone; some articles say it is a phobia of losing your mobile phone. Some even say it is an addiction; people are addicted to their iPhone or iPad. However, most authors are not aware of the concepts of addiction or phobia; when you have a closer look, both of them do not apply to a concept of "nomophobia." Just one example—I just read [an] article on the web. The author mentions that he "personally thinks it's getting worse with very little relief in sight with more and more people contracting the illness." Furthermore, he speaks of nomophobia and is switching later to internet addiction; he is citing only one study from Asia. The author himself is not a psychologist or psychiatrist, therefore the information I found in that article is really confusing for amateurs; nomophobia and internet addiction are different concepts.

In most cases, an over-use of the internet is connected to other psychological problems, such as depression or social anxiety.

What Is Addiction?

However, let's talk some real scientific facts—there are hundreds, if not thousands, more or less scientifically sound studies about internet addiction. I could go on and on with the facts, but summarized, there are no precise criteria regarding internet addiction. Therefore, every study has its own criteria. The prevalence rates of internet addiction range from somewhat 1% to up to 80% (!) in early studies. Recent studies found 3–5%, this seems to be a somewhat "real" rate of people having problems with a healthy internet use. However, talking about addiction: what is addiction anyway? Stating some simple criteria like "If checking and rechecking your phone comes as naturally to you as breathing, or if you feel anxious or restless any time your phone is not on or near you, you may have a technology addiction" is highly unprofessional. An addiction is the abuse or misuse of a psychoactive drug, or the repetition of a behavior despite adverse consequences (behavioral addiction only applies to gambling disorder). An addiction has to meet at least some of the following criteria (according to the *DSM*, the *Diagnostic and Statistical Manual* by the American Psychiatric Association) like:

- Tolerance towards the substance (need for an increasing amount of the substance; and a diminished effect with continued use of the same amount of the substance)

15

- Withdrawal symptoms

- The substance is often taken in larger amounts or over a longer period than was intended

- A persistent desire or unsuccessful efforts to cut down or control substance use

- Important social or recreational activities are given up or reduced because of substance use

- The substance use is continued despite knowledge of having a persistent or recurrent physical or psychological problem that is likely to have been caused or exacerbated by the substance

Nevertheless, some people are suffering from an "over-use" of the internet, they spend too much time online with negative effects on their social and work life. In most cases, people try to escape into virtual realities (to escape problems in real life), they try to enhance their mood (depression) or meet new people online (social anxieties). Furthermore, our studies revealed that a problematic internet use is often connected to a problematic online porn consuming.

Addiction Versus High Engagement

I do not have any doubts that some people do have problems with a healthy internet use, but the concept of addiction seems not to be the right one here. In most cases, an over-use of the internet is connected to other psychological problems, such as depression or social anxiety. Furthermore, I mentioned in another blog that most studies confuse high engagement with addiction. Being highly engaged in the internet or with your mobile phone or with computer games does *NOT* automatically mean you're addicted!

Even among high-level players of World of Warcraft, I only found 3% to be "addicted" (according to scientifically sound criteria), and there are significant differences between highly engaged and addicted players. An addiction factor loaded highly on items tapping interpersonal conflicts, withdrawal symptoms, relapse and reinstatement and behavioral salience criteria for behavioral addiction; an engagement factor tapped items concerning euphoria and cognitive salience criteria. Therefore, addiction criteria like euphoria and cognitive salience seem to be of limited use when it comes to a classification of internet gaming disorder, internet addiction or a problematic use of a mobile phone. Even the new version of the *DSM* includes internet gaming disorder without mentioning "addiction" and states "more profound research is needed before it is considered for inclusion as a psychological disorder in the *Diagnostic and Statistical Manual of Mental Disorders* (DSM) (American Psychiatric Association, 2013)."

The talk about nomophobia is a highly exaggerated media hype about an artificially created disorder.

What's a Phobia Got to Do with It?

The term nomophobia misleads many amateurs to believe it is an actually real disorder. But to be classified as a real disorder, a phobia has to meet at least some of the following criteria:

- A phobia is a marked and persistent fear that is excessive or unreasonable. It is cued by the presence or anticipation of a specific object or situation (e.g., flying, heights, animals, receiving an injection, seeing blood).

- Any exposure to the phobic stimulus almost invariably provokes an immediate anxiety response, which may take the form of a situationally bound or predisposed panic attack.

- The person recognizes that the fear is excessive or unreasonable.

- The phobic situation(s) is avoided or else is endured with intense anxiety or distress.

- The avoidance behavior or distress causes a significant impairment in the person's daily activities.

Discomfort Is Normal

About my mobile phone: I have everything connected with it. My social hubs, all my numbers, my favourite apps, my mobile banking account, my work emails, my favorite games. . . . With so much information stored on my phone (confidential emails, contact details, photos): Do I feel uncomfortable when I think about losing my phone? About other people reading all my private stuff? Of course I do, of course I feel somewhat anxious with the thoughts of losing my phone. If you apply this criteria, then I am a nomophobic. But is it a phobia? Very much not so. It is a normal behavior to have fears like this, losing a device with all my personal information stored on it makes me feel uncomfortable.

There seem to be a lot of people with problems concerning a healthy use of the internet or their mobile phone. Most studies connect this over-use with disorders like depression or social anxiety. Therefore, the over-use of technology can be a sign of psychological disorders, people try to escape their depression or social anxiety with the help of the internet or video games (if it makes people feel better, it is not necessarily always a bad thing). Nevertheless, in my opinion, the talk about nomophobia is a highly exaggerated media hype about an artificially created disorder.

3

Digital Multitasking Is Linked to Depression and Anxiety

Tara Haelle

As senior editor for the mental health referral service 1-800-Therapist.com, Tara Haelle leads a team of reporters in covering mental and behavioral health conditions.

A recent study examined whether using various forms of electronic media—such as smartphones, television, texting, or video games—at the same time (i.e., multitasking) is linked to mental health issues. The researchers found that multitasking among media types is linked to social anxiety and depression, although just the frequent use of different media types one at a time is not. Experts can't say that multitasking causes social anxiety and depression, only that there is a link between the two. More research is needed to determine the nature of the connection and to explore what it might mean for mental health.

Ever text messaged while watching TV? Or talked on the phone while playing a video game? Listened to iTunes while online? You're media multitasking—which is now linked to anxiety and depression.

A new study has found that individuals who frequently multitasked with media types were more likely to be anxious or depressed. That does not mean media multitasking makes you anxious or depressed. They don't know yet why the link is there.

But in the world of new media everywhere, it's a link worth exploring.

The study, led by Mark W. Becker, PhD, of the Department of Psychology at Michigan State University, looked at whether multitasking on media was linked to mental health issues. Dr. Becker and colleagues interviewed 319 undergraduates—more than two thirds female—about their media multitasking habits with a specific questionnaire.

The relationship between media multitasking and both depression and anxiety remained after the researchers took into account overall media use and personality traits like being neurotic or extroverted.

They were asked how many hours a week they used at least two types of media simultaneously. The media types included television, cell phones, text messaging, video games, personal computers, music, surfing the web and similar activities. The participants were also assessed with various psychology tools for their levels of anxiety, depression, neuroticism and extroversion.

An analysis of the results showed a link between frequently multitasking with different kinds of media and depression and social phobia.

The relationship between media multitasking and both depression and anxiety remained after the researchers took into account overall media use and personality traits like being neurotic or extroverted.

Frequency vs. Multitasking

Using a lot of different media frequently was not found to be related to social anxiety or depression, even though it was related to multitasking. It was only the multitasking that was tied to depression and anxiety.

However, this does not mean that media multitasking causes depression or anxiety. The link between the activity and the mental health condition could go either way.

One could cause the other, or there could be an underlying cause that affects both of them. In fact, it could even be that individuals with depression and/or anxiety are multitasking with different media to help cope with their condition.

"We don't know whether the media multitasking is causing symptoms of depression and social anxiety, or if it's that people who are depressed and anxious are turning to media multitasking as a form of distraction from their problems," Dr. Becker said.

It's worth noting that the idea of "media multitasking" is not necessarily new, said LuAnn Pierce, a social worker in Colorado and a dailyRx expert.

Flipping through a magazine while the television is on or while listening to music is also media multitasking and activities that people have been doing for decades. The difference now is that there are so many more types of media all around us.

Information Processing and Mental Health

"Now we read, listen to music and play games on our phones or computers, so it is easier to media multitask," Pierce said. "The use of digital technology and the MTV-style of taking in information in small, fast sound bytes has probably changed how we process information."

But the connection it shares with mental health is less clear overall, Pierce said.

"Understanding the correlation of media multitasking and anxiety or depression may not be easily resolved," she said. "I could see the relationship going in either direction—it will be interesting to see what future studies determine."

The authors said more research is needed to understand the relationship better and any possible causes. The study was published in the December issue of the journal *Cyberpsychology, Behavior and Social Networking*. Information regarding funding was unavailable, but the authors declared no conflicts of interest.

4

Social Media Can Cause or Worsen Anxiety Disorders

Dana Duong

Dana Duong is a producer at Anxiety.org as well as a copywriter, content marketer, and data analyst.

Many common online experiences put users at risk for anxiety. The various social media platforms that are popular today lend themselves to promoting anxiety disorders, such as social anxiety disorder (SAD), obsessive-compulsive disorder (OCD), and generalized anxiety disorder (GAD). Facebook, for example, is a prime source for SAD because for many users it generates a fear of missing out (FOMO) that leads to a feeling of being disconnected from social experiences. Reddit and Instagram contribute to SAD in different ways, while LinkedIn is often associated with GAD. Twitter and Pinterest, meanwhile, seem tailor-made for those who have OCD tendencies. Recognizing the ways in which social media promotes anxiety can help users navigate the pitfalls.

In both offline and online communities, we put ourselves at risk to anxiety inducing situations. Recently, physicians have been placing a lot of attention on social media as a trigger for anxiety. Take a look at these common online occurrences, and see how these social media platforms induce Social Anxiety Disorder (SAD), Obsessive Compulsive Disorder (OCD), and Generalized Anxiety Disorder (GAD). Some of these situations may sound too familiar to you.

Facebook

It's Friday night and you're at home. Today was slow, so you decided to leave the office early. Settled in your pajamas, you unlock your screen and open up Facebook. What's this? "John Brown and 7 others are at Local Pub." It looks like all of your coworkers decided to get drinks after work. Must have been a spontaneous decision, and since you had already gone home, there was no point in inviting you. However, you can't shake the feeling of loneliness and sadness. Then with a frown on your face, you like the post, type "tfti [thanks for the invite]," and post it. And from then on, you've stopped leaving the office early for fear of missing out on post-work festivities.

Those who Reddit are susceptible to SAD because of online rejection and judgment from strangers.

With the ability for users to upload pictures and videos, check in to locations, and tag friends in posts, Facebook might be the biggest online cause of SAD. The fear of missing out, or FOMO, refers to the social anxiety we get when we feel disconnected from social experiences. On Facebook, you can easily scroll through the feed and be updated on where your friends are, who they're with, and what they are doing—without you.

Reddit

Reddit loves cats. So in theory, if you post a picture of a tired kitten on r/aww, you'll surely break 1,000 karma. But right after you post, your cat picture is downvoted to -38, and people fill your inbox with comments saying that they've already seen this a million times. You're left with negative karma, a reputation of being unoriginal, and a growing fear of sharing ever again.

Those who Reddit are susceptible to SAD because of online rejection and judgment from strangers. Unlike most platforms, Reddit is a more anonymous form of social media that focuses on forum style posts. Each post is public and all users can "upvote" and "downvote" posts. This means that complete strangers can like or dislike whatever you contribute. Sometimes, posts will be downvoted into negative numbers. And since Reddit users tend to stay anonymous, people are more inclined to dish out harsh judgment for the sake of humor. Those who cannot take jokes with a grain of salt should stay away.

Instagram

You snap a picture of yourself, slap on the Walden filter, type "#selfie," and share it. Hours pass, and no one has liked your picture. You second-guess how good you think you look, and instantly feel unattractive.

Are you Instafamous? Accounts that attract the most traffic seem to be amateur models. After looking at accounts with more than 100,000 followers, you can't help but feel insecure about the popularity of your pictures. Instagram may be increasing the number of those with SAD with its popularity-based community. Photos left unliked give users a sense of, "Why doesn't anyone like my pictures?" or "No one seems interested in me." Users obsessing over selfies may also suffer from Body Dysmorphic Disorder.

The phenomenon of live-tweeting has led to people obsessively posting about every single facet of their lives, but excessive Twitter use can easily dip into OCD territory.

Social Media and Obsessive Compulsive Disorder (OCD)

Pinterest

You've just created a Pinterest. The homepage opens up and overwhelms your visual senses with crisp photos of cute outfits, delectable desserts, and impressive DIY [do-it yourself] projects. Before you know it, you're scrolling up and down, pinning left and right. But then you realize that you've pinned a picture of a lilac gradient garden onto your Homemade Recipes Board. Fury fills you as you go to edit your board and restore order.

Pinterest addicts show signs of OCD. Pinterest allows users to post pictures on virtual boards. These boards generally have themes like "hobbies" or "food." Collecting photos and meticulously organizing them onto boards reflect obsessive behaviors. A main symptom of OCD is obsession. A common obsession is the necessity to have things in a particular order. On Pinterest, addicts tend to obsess over the quality of their pins and organization of their boards.

Twitter

Wake up. Tweet, "Goodmorning #twitterverse!" Brush teeth. Tweet, "Bye morning breath." Cook breakfast. Tweet, "Why am I trying? Just another meal for one." Read Justin Bieber's latest tweet. Tweet, "@justinbieber Go back to Canada!"

In 140 characters or less, you can tweet whatever's on your mind. The phenomenon of live-tweeting has led to people obsessively posting about every single facet of their lives, but excessive Twitter use can easily dip into OCD territory. Users seem to find relief when they tweet, get retweeted, or gain new followers. People also use Twitter to keep up with news and celebrities. Many celebrities and companies use Twitter as an outreach to their fan base. This means you can directly complain to Taco Bell about your soggy CrunchWrap Supreme or stay up-to-date with the mundane lives of your favorite celebrities. Come up for air in between tweets to avoid the pitfalls of Twitter-induced OCD.

Social Media and General Anxiety Disorder (GAD)

LinkedIn

Upon opening up LinkedIn, a red flag tells you that two people viewed your profile this week. Who, exactly? Because you don't have premium, you can only see one of the two: the hiring manager of a big start-up. But you haven't been on LinkedIn in months. When you look at your profile, to your horror, you no-tice a typo, a Yahoo email address, and only four lonely connec-tions. The hiring manager probably didn't want to connect with you because of your lack of professionalism. After frantically fix-ing and optimizing your profile, you retreat to your room to cry out of embarrassment.

For many, LinkedIn has successfully connected them to important people in the business world and served as a portal to new jobs. Unique to LinkedIn, users can see who has viewed their profile. Knowing which powerful CEO looks at your profile can cause constant worry about the quality of your ac-count, as well as the connections you've made so far. This continuous fear is a symptom of GAD. Your LinkedIn profile may determine the success of your career, and that's why it's making you anxious.

5

Cyberbullying Creates Dangerous Stress and Anxiety

Sameer Hinduja and Justin W. Patchin

Sameer Hinduja is a professor at Florida Atlantic University, and Justin W. Patchin is a professor at the University of Wisconsin-Eau Claire. Together, they speak on the causes and consequences of cyberbullying and have written six books and numerous articles on teen technology use and misuse.

When young people use computers, smartphones, and other electronic devices to harass, threaten, humiliate, or otherwise taunt their peers, it is called "cyberbullying." The range of behaviors that constitute cyberbullying can vary widely, from sending nasty text messages and posting hurtful social media updates, to uploading unauthorized photos or videos to the web, or even creating bogus websites in order to ridicule or shame someone. Targets of cyberbullying often experience stress and anxiety and are frequently afraid or embarrassed to go to school or be seen by their peers. Like regular bullying, cyberbullying can have serious consequences, including depression, anxiety, low self-esteem, suicidal thoughts, and academic problems, among others.

Kids have been bullying each other for generations. The latest generation, however, has been able to utilize technology to expand their reach and the extent of their harm. This phenomenon is being called *cyberbullying*, defined as: *"willful and repeated harm inflicted through the use of comput-*

ers, cell phones, and other electronic devices." Basically, we are referring to incidents where adolescents use technology to harass, threaten, humiliate, or otherwise hassle their peers. For example, youth can send hurtful text messages to others or spread rumors using smartphones or tablets. Teens have also created web pages, videos, and profiles on social media platforms making fun of others. With mobile devices, adolescents have taken pictures in a bedroom, a bathroom, or another location where privacy is expected, and posted or distributed them online. Others have recorded unauthorized videos of other kids and uploaded them for the world to see, rate, tag, and discuss. Still others are embracing anonymous apps or chat functionality on gaming networks to tear down or humiliate others.

Estimates of the number of youth who experience cyberbullying vary widely (ranging from 10–40% or more), depending on the age of the group studied and how cyberbullying is formally defined.

What Are the Effects of Cyberbullying?

There are many detrimental outcomes associated with cyberbullying that reach into the real world. First, many targets report feeling depressed, sad, angry, and frustrated. As one teenager stated: "It makes me hurt both physically and mentally. It scares me and takes away all my confidence. It makes me feel sick and worthless." Those who are victimized by cyberbullying also reveal that they are often afraid or embarrassed to go to school. In addition, research has revealed a link between cyberbullying and low self-esteem, family problems, academic difficulties, school violence, and various delinquent behaviors. Finally, cyberbullied youth also report having suicidal thoughts, and there have been a number of examples in the United States and abroad where youth who were victimized ended up taking their own lives.

Where Does Cyberbullying Commonly Occur?

Cyberbullying occurs across a variety of venues and mediums in cyberspace, and it shouldn't come as a surprise that it occurs most often where teenagers congregate. Initially, many kids hung out in chat rooms, and as a result that is where most harassment took place. In recent years, most youth have been drawn to social media (such as Instagram, Snapchat, and Twitter) and video-sharing sites (such as YouTube). This trend has led to increased reports of cyberbullying occurring in those environments. Voice chat, textual chat, and texting via phones or tablets also can provide an environment in which hate and harm is expressed. We are also seeing it happen with portable gaming devices, in 3-D virtual worlds and social gaming sites, and in newer interactive apps like Yik Yak, Secret, and Whisper.

Cyberbullying by the Numbers

Estimates of the number of youth who experience cyberbullying vary widely (ranging from 10–40% or more), depending on the age of the group studied and how cyberbullying is formally defined. In our research, we inform students that cyberbullying is when someone "repeatedly makes fun of another person online or repeatedly picks on another person through email or text message or when someone posts something online about another person that they don't like." Using this definition, about 25 percent of the over 10,000 randomly-selected 11–18 year-olds we have surveyed over the last seven years have said that they have been cyberbullied at some point in their lifetimes. About 17 percent admitted to cyberbullying others during their lifetime. In our most recent study of middle-school youth from January of 2014, 12 percent said they had been cyberbullied while 4 percent said they had cyberbullied others within the previous 30 days.

Cyberbullying vs. Traditional Bullying

While often similar in terms of form and technique, cyberbullying and bullying have many differences that can make the former even more devastating. With the former, victims may not know who the bully is, or why they are being targeted. The cyberbully can cloak his or her identity behind a computer or phone using anonymous email addresses or pseudonymous screen names. Second, the hurtful actions of a cyberbully are viral; that is, a large number of people (at school, in the neighborhood, in the city, in the world!) can be involved in the victimization, or at least find out about the incident with a few keystrokes or touchscreen impressions. It seems, then, that the pool of potential victims, offenders, and witnesses/bystanders is limitless.

Some kids feel free to post or send whatever they want while online without considering how that content can inflict pain.

Third, it is often easier to be cruel using technology because cyberbullying can be done from a physically distant location, and the bully doesn't have to see the immediate response by the target. In fact, some teens simply might not recognize the serious harm they are causing because they are sheltered from the victim's response. Finally, while parents and teachers are doing a better job supervising youth at school and at home, many adults don't have the technological know-how (or time!) to keep track of what teens are up to online. As a result, a victim's experiences may be missed and a bully's actions may be left unchecked. Even if bullies are identified, many adults find themselves unprepared to adequately respond.

Why Is Cyberbullying Becoming a Major Issue?

Cyberbullying is a growing problem because increasing numbers of kids are using and have completely embraced online interactivity. A remarkable 95% of teens in the US are online, and three-fourths (74%) access the Internet on their mobile device. They do so for school work, to keep in touch with their friends, to play games, to learn about celebrities, to share their digital creations, or for many other reasons. Because the online communication tools have become such a tremendous part of their lives, it is not surprising that some youth have decided to use the technology to be malicious or menacing towards others. The fact that teens are connected to technology 24/7 means they are susceptible to victimization (and able to act on mean intentions toward others) around the clock. As alluded to, is also easier to be hateful using typed words rather than spoken words face-to-face. And because some adults have been slow to respond to cyberbullying, many cyberbullies feel that there are little to no consequences for their actions. Many even feel that there is little chance of detection and identification, let alone sanction.

Cyberbullying crosses all geographical boundaries. The Internet has really opened up the whole world to users who access it on a broad array of devices, and for the most part this has been a good thing (a really good thing!). Nevertheless, because of the issues previously discussed, some kids feel free to post or send whatever they want while online without considering how that content can inflict pain—and sometimes cause severe psychological and emotional wounds.

Obstacles in the Fight to Stop Cyberbullying

There are two primary challenges today that make it difficult to prevent cyberbullying. First, even though this problem has been around for well over a decade, some people still don't see the harm associated with it. Some attempt to dismiss or disregard cyberbullying because there are "more serious forms of aggression to worry about." While it is true that there are many issues facing adolescents, parents, teachers, and law enforcement today, we first need to accept that cyberbullying is one such problem that will only get more serious if ignored.

We must remember that kids are not sociopaths—they are just kids who sometimes lack empathy and make mistakes.

The other challenge relates to who is willing to step up and take responsibility for responding to inappropriate use of technology. Parents often say that they don't have the technical skills to keep up with their kids' online behavior, and that schools should be covering it in detail during class time and through other programming. Educators are often doing their part through policies, curricula, training, and assemblies, but sometimes don't know when and how to intervene in online behaviors that occur away from school but still involve their students. Finally, law enforcement is hesitant to get involved unless there is clear evidence of a crime or a significant threat to someone's physical safety. As a result, cyberbullying incidents either slip through the cracks, are dealt with too formally, are dealt with too informally, or are otherwise mismanaged. At that point, the problem behaviors often continue and escalate because they aren't adequately or appropriately addressed. Based on these challenges, we collectively need to create an environment where kids feel comfortable talking with adults about this problem and feel confident that meaningful steps will be taken to resolve the situation. We also need to get everyone involved—kids, parents, educators, counselors, youth leaders, law enforcement, social media companies, and the community at large. It will take a concerted and comprehensive effort from all stakeholders to make a meaningful difference in reducing cyberbullying. . . .

Kids need to learn that inappropriate online actions will not be tolerated. Get them to understand that technology use and access is a privilege, and not a right—and with those privileges comes certain responsibilities that *must* be respected.

If a parent discovers that their child is cyberbullying others, they should first communicate how that behavior inflicts harm and causes pain in the real world as well as in cyberspace. We must remember that kids are not sociopaths—they are just kids who sometimes lack empathy and make mistakes. That said, there are ramifications for every choice they made. Depending on the level of seriousness of the incident, and whether it seems that the child has realized the hurtful nature of his or her behavior, consequences should be firmly applied (and escalated if the behavior continues). Moving forward, it is essential that parents pay even greater attention to the technology use of their child to make sure that they have internalized the lesson and are continually acting in responsible ways. Not only should they not be doing the wrong thing, they should be doing the right thing online!

A positive on-campus environment will go a long way in reducing the frequency of many problematic behaviors at school, including bullying and harassment.

The Role of Schools

The most important preventive step that schools can take is to educate the school community about responsible Internet use. Students need to know that all forms of bullying are wrong and that those who engage in harassing or threatening behaviors will be subject to discipline. It is therefore essential to discuss issues related to appropriate online communications in various areas of the general curriculum. To be sure, these messages should be reinforced in classes that regularly utilize technology. Signage also should be posted around campus to remind students of the rules of acceptable use. In general, it is crucial to establish and maintain an environment of respect and integrity where violations result in informal or formal sanction.

Furthermore, school district personnel should review their harassment and bullying policies to ensure that it allows for the discipline of students who engage in cyberbullying. If their policy covers it, cyberbullying incidents that occur at school—or that originate off campus but ultimately result in a substantial disruption of the learning environment—are well within a school's legal authority to intervene. The school then needs to make it clear to students, parents, and all staff that these behaviors are unacceptable and will be subject to discipline. . . .

Cyberbullying and School Climate

The benefits of a positive school climate have been identified through much research over the last thirty years. It contributes to more consistent attendance, higher student achievement, and other desirable student outcomes. Though limited, the research done on school climate and traditional bullying also underscores its importance in preventing peer conflict. One of our recent studies found that students who experienced cyberbullying (both those who were victims and those who admitted to cyberbullying others) perceived a poorer climate at their school than those who had not experienced cyberbullying. Youth were asked whether they "enjoy going to school," "feel safe at school," "feel that teachers at their school really try to help them succeed," and "feel that teachers at their school care about them." Those who admitted to cyberbullying others or who were the target of cyberbullying were less likely to agree with those statements.

Overall, it is critical for educators to develop and promote a safe and respectful school climate—one marked by shared and palpable feelings of connectedness, belongingness, peer respect, morale, safety, and even school spirit. A positive on-campus environment will go a long way in reducing the frequency of many problematic behaviors at school, including bullying and harassment. In this setting, teachers must demonstrate emotional support, a warm and caring atmosphere, a strong focus on academics and learning, and a fostering of healthy self-esteem. As mentioned, it is crucial that the school seeks to create and promote an atmosphere where certain conduct [is] not tolerated—by students and staff alike. In schools with healthy climates, students know what is appropriate and what is not.

6

Researching Health Symptoms Online Can Cause Unnecessary Anxiety

Ben Meghreblian

Ben Meghreblian was a graduate student in experimental psychology at the University of Oxford at the time this article was written. He is also a coauthor of the study referred to in the viewpoint.

Most Internet users search for information about health conditions online, but it may do them more harm than good. Even when searching for common symptoms, search results tend to highlight serious and rare conditions rather than more probable culprits, and there are often problems with the quality, accuracy, and credibility of health websites. People who have health anxiety, the fear that one has a serious illness despite the absence of a physical problem or medical diagnosis, are especially prone to looking for health information online and to experiencing increased anxiety when they find information that supports their fears. A study of the issue found that searching for health information online "may exacerbate health anxiety."

Wondering what that rash on your arm is? If the cough you've had for a few days warrants making an appointment to see your doctor/physician? If you've ever used the internet to answer these sort of questions then you're in the 60–80% of internet users who regularly do so.

In theory this is a great idea—you get access to the collective knowledge of medicine, and you don't get kicked out of the appointment room after 15 minutes.

However, there are a few problems—research tell us that:

- If you use a general search engine such as Google to search for non-specific symptoms, you will get a disproportionate amount of information on serious and rare medical explanations.

- 70% of those who initially search for common, innocuous symptoms progress to searching for information on rare, more serious conditions.

- There are significant problems with the quality, accuracy, and completeness of health websites, potentially exposing users to conflicting or confusing information.

- Most users fail to check basic credentials (e.g. source validity and date of publication) and view online health information as reliable and of "good" or "excellent" quality.

Studies suggest that the lifetime prevalence rate of health anxiety is as high as 5%.

Put all those together and you've got a potential problem. Now imagine if you're someone with high levels of health anxiety. OK, wait a minute. . . .

What Is Health Anxiety?

Health anxiety is characterised by a preoccupation with either the fear of having, or belief that one already has a serious physical illness, in the absence of organic pathology (i.e. there is no physical problem). Those with high levels of health anxiety make catastrophic misinterpretations of benign bodily sensations and become fixated on their suspected illness, seeking repeated reassurance and medical consultations to investigate the perceived illness. However, their assumptions and expectations of medical consultations, combined with their misinterpretations of both test results (which show no evidence of illness) and the well-intentioned reassurance from medical staff, lead health anxious patients to enter a cycle of reassurance seeking and significant psychosocial distress.

In addition to the personal distress and impairment that health anxious individuals experience, they also place a significant burden on health services, utilising an estimated 41–78% more health care per year. Studies suggest that the lifetime prevalence rate of health anxiety is as high as 5%, with as many as 9% of patients in primary care meeting criteria, although diagnoses are rarely given, mostly due to issues of stigmatisation and/or patients' presentations being better explained by a wider psychiatric disorder.

The Study

K. Muse et al. (2012) were interested in examining different ways in which individuals with high levels of health anxiety sought health information online compared to those with low levels of health anxiety, the impact of seeking out this information, and their perceptions of the information.

They used the Short Health Anxiety Inventory (SHAI) to determine participants' levels of health anxiety, and took the top and bottom quartiles of scores to represent high vs. low levels of health anxiety. To investigate internet use, they administered a new questionnaire which sought to examine:

1. If participants used the internet to seek health information and reasons for not doing so

2. The frequency and duration of any searching online for health information

3. The effect of searching online on participants' distress and health anxiety

4. The type of health information sought and the sources used

5. The perceived accuracy of online health information

So next time you're wondering about a rash or that cough, [it] may be best not to start googling!

The Results

- A greater proportion of those with high levels of health anxiety sought health information online, with a significantly greater proportion of those with low levels of health anxiety saying they had "no need to look up health information."

- Those with high levels of health anxiety sought health information online significantly more frequently than those with low levels, and this pattern was the same for duration of time spent searching.

- Those with high levels of health anxiety rated the impact of searching for health information online as significantly more distressing and as having a significantly more negative impact on how anxious they felt about their health, compared to those with low levels.

- A significantly greater proportion of those with high levels of health anxiety reported searching for information on "diagnosed" and "undiagnosed" medical conditions and "looking for descriptions of other people's experiences of illness." As for the source of information, the only difference found was that a significantly greater proportion of those with high levels of health anxiety reported using message boards/support groups for health information.

- There was no difference in perceived accuracy of health information online, with both groups rating it to be moderately accurate.

In conclusion, to quote the abstract:

"This preliminary data suggests that searching for health information online may exacerbate health anxiety."

So next time you're wondering about a rash or that cough, [it] may be best not to start googling!

7

Digital Overload: Too Much Technology Takes a Toll

Ned Smith

Freelance writer Ned Smith is a former senior writer at Sweeney Vesty, an international consulting firm, and vice president of communications for iQuest Analytics.

The promise of the digital age has been that constant connectedness will increase productivity and effectiveness, but the opposite has turned out to be true. The constant onslaught of information from smart phones, computers, and other digital devices has actually decreased productivity, creativity, and the quality of personal relationships. Information overload and the multitasking required by today's digital demands make people feel like there is too much to do and that life is spinning out of control. Acknowledging that one has a problem with overconsumption of digital technology is the first step toward reducing the negative impacts of technology use.

It's the great irony of the digital age. It seems that the more we do, the less that we get done. Many experts believe it's our own digital dust that's dragging us down.

Our constant connectedness, the beeping and buzzing and bleeping digital devices we carry around, aren't just causing us to become mega-multitaskers, they are also taking a social and financial toll.

Basex, a research firm that specializes in technical issues in the workplace, reckons that information overload is responsible for economic losses of $900 billion a year at work.

The real due bill, though, may be for the damage this busyness has inflicted on our productivity, creativity and the quality of our relationships.

"I think this 24/7 layer of connectedness we've added has really ramped up the feeling that life is going out of control," said William Powers, author of *Hamlet's Blackberry*, a cautionary tale about the digital din of our own making.

As with most addictions, acknowledging that there's a problem is the first step toward finding a cure.

The first warning sign is usually a heightened sense of having too much going on that requires a constant toggling of our attention, he said.

"You don't really know how addicted you are," Powers told *BusinessNewsDaily*. "You're skating on the surface of your day. We're not built to handle that onslaught of information."

As with most addictions, acknowledging that there's a problem is the first step toward finding a cure.

"You have to recognize what's going on," he said.

Conquering Cyber Overload

Dr. Joanne Cantor, a professor at the University of Wisconsin-Madison, has faced that issue firsthand. A self-described "recovering cyber addict," she found herself tethered to e-mail and unable to rein in her online multitasking. She was getting less done, working more slowly and unable to concentrate.

After investigating research on how the brain works under information overload, she cut back on her media connectedness.

"Things turned around dramatically," she said. "I became a zealot."

Her book, *Conquer CyberOverload,* grew out of that research and the workshops she subsequently conducted to coach people on how to regain control of their lives by scaling back their use of digital devices.

Neither Cantor nor Powers are Luddites, advocating that we purge our lives of electronic devices. In the first place, it would be impossible—we can't roll back time and the workplace to an earlier, less-connected era. It simply is no longer there.

Equally important, both say, these devices have greatly enhanced our capabilities and shrunk our world in a positive way. Our goal should be to regain control of our lives and how we use these devices. Are they controlling us or do we control them?

One well-known figure from history who wrestled with the impact of technology, Powers said, was Henry David Thoreau. In Thoreau's case, the encroaching technology was the telegraph, which made instantaneous communications possible.

"But lo! Men have become the tools of their tools," Thoreau wrote in *Walden Pond.* "We are in great haste to construct a magnetic telegraph from Maine to Texas; but Maine and Texas, it may be, have nothing important to communicate."

It's not enough [to] control our devices . . . we need to control our time as well.

Setting Boundaries with Technology

"You own your gadgets," Cantor said. "They don't own you. They're like newborn babies always clamoring for your attention."

You need to know when to say no, she said.

A good place to start, she said, is by learning to take a more sequential approach to life.

"Limit your multitasking," she said. "Do one thing at a time. You'll find you actually save time."

Cantor cited research conducted at Stanford University that showed that multitasking was highly over-rated and often counterproductive.

It's not enough [to] control our devices, she added, we need to control our time as well.

"Be the master of your interruptions," she said. "Don't be on call for everyone 24/7. Don't let yourself be an all-day receptionist. You can Twitter your life away if you respond every time a response comes in. You need to set boundaries. It's very hard to do at first."

It's an incremental learning process, she said. You don't need to do it all day. Try it for 15 minutes to begin with, she recommends, or wait until you're ready before checking your email.

By adopting a more measured approach to your email, she said, you may also sidestep "sender's regret" when you're too quick to hit the reply button.

"The benefit of all this technology is a two-edged sword," she said. "The ease of use comes back to bite you."

"Be both the grasshopper and the ant," Cantor suggested.

Time to Recharge

Being a workaholic doesn't, in fact, pay off in terms of increased productivity, she said. Just like the battery in your laptop, you need to recharge. Play and leisure are as important in the creative process as hard work.

"Research shows that information overload interferes with your ability to think outside the box," Cantor said.

For Powers, the solution that works for him and his family is an "Internet Sabbath." They shut off their modem on Friday and restore the connection on Monday. This family ritual, he said, is now in its fourth year.

"When we return to our digital lives on Monday, we're better at it," he said. "That space helps me as a digital person. We have to calibrate our own connectedness, and that's going to be different for every person."

8

Using Technology Mindfully Can Reduce Anxiety from Digital Overload

Anastasia Papazafeiropoulou

Anastasia Papazafeiropoulou is director of postgraduate studies at Brunei University in London.

Many people feel overwhelmed, anxious, or depressed by the information overload that comes from being connected to the Internet 24/7, but that doesn't need to be the case. If users pay attention to the way they interact with technology and make themselves deliberately aware of how it is affecting them and those around them, it can still have a positive influence in their lives. Setting personal boundaries for technology use, such as considering whether a text, tweet, or e-mail is really necessary, is a good place to start. With social media, examining one's intentions before interacting with others is a good habit to develop. If one's use of technology is done with mindfulness, not absentmindedness, it can have positive effects in many areas.

Information overload has become an everyday experience for anyone who works with computers, owns a smartphone or waits at a bus stop with minute-by-minute updates about arrival times.

And this information overload has been cited as a major factor in the rise of stress-related diseases. Some advocate a digital detox as the antidote to the curse of email, social media and constant communication but for many, that just isn't practical.

Others are turning to traditional mindfulness meditation techniques as a way of managing their digital dependence without having to switch off from their everyday lives entirely. It's seen as a way to calm the mind and help the body to cope with the overwhelming amount of data coming our way from all different directions and sources.

Once you are used to receiving a constant stream of news, you start to feel lost without it. That can cause anxiety and depression.

As long ago as June 1983, *Time* magazine ran a cover feature on stress as a modern anxiety. Three decades later, answers to the problem are being put forward by that same magazine. A February 2014 issue of *Time* featured a cover that read: "The mindful revolution: The science of finding focus in a stressed-out, multitasking culture."

In 2014, *Time* readers, like many others, want practical solutions to their stress. We answer work emails while waiting in a supermarket queue, we pay bills while preparing dinner and we follow our favourite celebrity's tweets while we eat it. We can begin to feel like we couldn't escape all the stimuli even if we wanted to.

Answer your work email on the weekend often enough and you can feel like it's expected of you to do so all the time. Once you are used to receiving a constant stream of news, you start to feel lost without it. That can cause anxiety and depression.

Managing Mindfully

Mindfulness has been described as "a moment-to-moment attention to present experience with a stance of open curiosity."

It's our ability to deliberately become more aware of the present moment and less caught up in our regrets for the past or anxiety for the future.

Mindfulness has been studied extensively in the medical domain as a potential tool in managing a number of conditions such as anxiety and help with recovery from illness.

Mindfulness is using the brain's ability to change and became stronger when trained accordingly, an ability called neuroplasticity, which is comparable to a muscle changing as a result of physical exercise. Mindfulness Based Stress Reduction is a training programme developed by Jon-Kabat-Zinn at the University of Massachusetts Medical Center that draws on this trait and aims to complement medical treatment for chronic pain and stress related disorders.

Social media, which feeds our desire for constant information sharing, is another practice that, when done mindfully, can become a fruitful social interaction rather than a mindless disruption.

Mindfulness Is Good for Business

Then there is the use of mindfulness as a business tool. Mindful leadership, for example, is often viewed as a way to help individuals and organisations to be successful while also being kind and thoughtful. The search inside yourself programme developed by Google's Chade-Meng Tan, is an example. Tan urges people who take his course to cultivate emotional awareness as a way to handle the stresses of work. The trend has spread and mindfulness meditation has been common practice at companies across Silicon Valley.

Away from Silicon Valley, there are small steps we can take to bring mindfulness to our digital lives. E-mail is a good place to start. It is believed that most people overindulge in mindless emailing as it is considered a quick and convenient way to communicate.

In a study conducted by the University of Glasgow and Modeuro Consulting, executives at the utility company London Power were asked to be more mindful about the emails they send to staff and to think twice every time they were about to hit the send button. As a result, email around the office was reduced by half during the study, leading the researchers to conclude that the company could save 11,000 working hours a year as a result.

Mindful emailing includes practices such as taking three breaths before responding to a stressful email and also considering the psychological effect that the email will have to the recipient or recipients.

Pausing for Thought

Social media, which feeds our desire for constant information sharing, is another practice that, when done mindfully, can become a fruitful social interaction rather than a mindless disruption.

Mindful use of social media includes checking our intentions before uploading a feed, being authentic in our communications and choosing the time we spend on social media rather than falling in to it. That way, we give it some of our spare time rather than allowing it to creep around the fringes of our whole life, potentially disrupting us at any time.

These are all relatively small steps but rely on the user of a technology to pause for thought as they go. It's a simple technique that many think has had significant results in a variety of contexts. We've been coping with our very modern malady for decades, perhaps we are finally making some progress.

9

The Internet Doesn't Overwhelm Most Americans

Chandra Johnson

Chandra Johnson is a staff writer for the Deseret News National *newspaper, based in Utah.*

A recent study found that most people don't feel overwhelmed by the volume of online information they encounter and instead feel they have benefited from it. The Pew Research Center polled one thousand American adults and only 26 percent reported experiencing information overload. Most respondents (87 percent) said that the Internet helps them learn new things, and most (72 percent) also said they liked having so much information available to them. Experts question, however, whether people truly are better informed or just think they are. The term "information overload" itself is also subject to scrutiny, and some suggest that it is not the volume of information that causes people to feel overwhelmed but rather the expectation to constantly engage with it.

A new survey from the Pew Research Center found that the majority of Americans say they do not feel overwhelmed by how much information they can get online. Instead, they say they've benefited from it.

The survey quizzed more than 1,000 adults this past September [2014] about how the Internet makes them feel and impacts their lives. About 87 percent of the respondents said the Internet helped them learn new things, and 72 percent said they liked having so much information, while just 26 percent said they felt "overloaded."

The report stated that variances in enthusiasm about the amount of online information were small—women were a little more likely than men to report feeling overwhelmed (30 percent vs. 21 percent), as were Internet users over age 50 (30 percent vs. 22 percent for those 49 and younger).

"The answer that we got is such an American answer. Given the choice, people like more choice and prefer abundance to scarcity," survey author Lee Rainie said. "Even though information is hyper-abundant, people probably feel they can find the stuff they want when they want it because search engines are so effective."

Just because we have access doesn't mean we use it [information] in a beneficial way.

The results aren't a surprise to Harvard University's Dr. David Weinberger, who thinks people are excited at the availability of information rather than intimidated.

"I hear people saying they're so happy to be able to get information so quickly. Overall, that's a good thing," Weinberger said. "What you used to have to do to get information now sounds Medieval. Now, you pull out a mobile phone and get an answer."

Psychologist Jim Taylor says the survey results are a sign of America's tolerance for a lot of information, and that's not necessarily something to celebrate.

"The norm has changed and overloaded is the new normal for people," Taylor said. "But just because we have access doesn't mean we use it in a beneficial way."

Informed or Exposed?

Rainie said he was most surprised at how many Americans feel the Internet helps them—and how many others, like students—learn new things.

But Taylor and University of Texas at Austin psychologist Art Markman say they worry about how much Americans learn online vs. how much they think they learn.

"Most people believe they understand the way the world works better than they actually do. Just being exposed to something makes you think you understand it," Markman said. "Because there's so much information available, there's a tendency for us to take that information in 3-minute bites. That doesn't give us opportunity to really learn."

To really learn something, Taylor says, people have to not only take in information, but process it—a crucial step he says people miss in the break-neck speed of the Internet.

"Information is just a tool and it only has value to the extent that it's able to be processed and integrated. Looking at so much information at a time can't necessarily allow that," Taylor said. "We need mindfulness when we take in information not only for our psychological health, but also for creativity."

To solve the problem? Engage with online content rather than just scanning it. Research topics rather than taking headlines at face value. Don't rely only on texting to communicate.

It may be that "information overload" is a way of expressing some free-floating anxiety about the Internet in general.

"If you take time to really read and make time for a conversation rather than a quick email or text, you provide more opportunities for real depth in thinking," Markman said. "That's something we've lost along the way."

Defining "Overload"

Weinberger says part of the reason people might say they don't feel overwhelmed by information is because the term itself is so ill-defined.

"It may be that 'information overload' is a way of expressing some free-floating anxiety about the Internet in general," Weinberger said. "But if we're saying that it has some deleterious effects, we have yet to find these people."

Weinberger said the term "information overload" was coined in the wake of another term from the 1950s, "sensory overload"—when people worried that too much exposure to new media like television and rock music would inundate the senses so much that a person would faint.

"As computers became more pervasive in mainstream culture, they called it 'information overload'—a term with very little meaning," Weinberger said. "It's the same reason we don't hear about sensory overload much anymore—it doesn't seem to be a real thing."

Weinberger theorized that the term "information overload" originated out of fear of change. When the ability for anyone to publish and read anything they wanted online became a reality, Weinberger said, the publishing industry went through culture shock.

"The term originated with people who once controlled publication and took pride in filtering information for us," Weinberger said. "I think this survey shows that these people felt threatened and they warned us, 'If we're not there to tell you what to look at, you'll suffer from information overload.'"

The New Normal

Weinberger says Pew's results don't surprise him given the way people think about being overwhelmed online. It's usually not about information, Weinberger said, but obligation.

"I hear people talking about feeling oppressed specifically with social media, where there is always more to read and an obligation to connect," Weinberger said. "That expectation for response—on email, on social media—can create overload."

While the term is murky, that doesn't mean people aren't feeling overwhelmed, as Rainie pointed out.

"There are people who do feel overwhelmed. It's just not the majority," Rainie said. "People are making accommodations and adjustments to the new reality of things. This is the new normal for lots of people and they seem to have become accustomed to it."

Navigating that new reality means creating personal boundaries, Markman said.

"Almost every device has an off switch," Markman said. "Run a little experiment: If you shut your cell off for a couple of hours, does it have a negative impact on your life? Rather than just taking the world as it is, impose yourself on the world a little bit."

10

Activity Tracking Can Cause Anxiety and Hyper-Vigilance

Mary E. Pritchard

Mary E. Pritchard is a professor in the psychology department at Boise State University in Idaho.

Activity tracking devices are touted as being a good way to manage weight and increase physical activity. For some people they can indeed be helpful, but for many others they can promote anxiety or dangerous behaviors due to unhealthy use of the devices. Activity trackers enable hyper-vigilance about the amount of exercise one engages in and/or the number of calories one consumes, and that can be especially problematic for people who have eating disorders or other sorts of body image problems. Signals that a person's fitness tracker use might be unhealthy include increased reliance on the device, anxiety prompted by its disuse or unavailability, and increasing amounts of time spent tracking physical activities and calories consumed.

Nike, Fitbit, Polar, Soleus, Jawbone, Garmin, even LG—it seems many manufacturers are cashing in on the fitness tracker craze. If you don't want to purchase a device, no worries, there's an app for that! MyFitnessPal, RunKeeper, Diet Tracker, Fitter Fitness, Map My Fitness, Fitness Buddy, the list goes on. . . .

Are they useful? Sure! They are great for those who really have no idea how many calories they are burning during an activity or how many calories are in different foods they are eating. They can also really help those in need of a motivational tool to keep them going.

But there's a downside. I was recently asked by a reporter whether there were any potential negatives to using a Fitness Tracker or Fitness App. My answer? Absolutely.

Tracking everything you put in your mouth for weeks on end might get a little tedious and obsessive for some.

I was talking to a client of mine about this the other day. She recently joined a weight loss support group where using MyFitnessPal was recommended so that everyone in the group could see each other's progress and encourage each other to stay on track when they didn't eat right or engage in any physical activity. At first, she was excited about the prospect of being held accountable by her app and her group members. But on day two, she realized something: 1) she wasn't being honest about her food intake or her activity level because 'other people were watching', which kind of defeated the purpose of tracking in the first place, and 2) she found herself anxious and thinking about either bingeing or restricting to compensate for her fear of being judged by those in her weight loss group.

Accountability vs. Anxiety

And that really is the dark side of fitness trackers. For many, they can be a very useful tool, but if you have or have ever had a tendency toward an eating disorder, they can be a nightmare. That 'accountability' can push you over the edge into danger zone—and it happens so quickly and easily that you may not realize it at first.

Which begs the question: Should you be tracking at all? I get this question a lot. And, again, it depends. I think if you have no tendency toward any type of eating disordered mentality, tracking your workouts or your food intake for a little while can be very motivating; but tracking everything you put in your mouth for weeks on end might get a little tedious and obsessive for some.

Warning Signs

So what's healthy use of fitness devices and apps and what's a warning sign?

I tend to use the same criteria for addiction to fitness devices as I do for addiction to exercise:

1. *Tolerance*—either a need for increased reliance on the app/tracker or increasing amounts of exercise or decreased amounts of food because using the tracker makes you feel like you should be doing more and more

2. *Withdrawal*—you either get anxious when you can't use your tracker or have to use the app to avoid the anxiety you know you will experience if you don't use it

3. *Intention Effect*—spend more time using the tracker/app than you intended—get caught up in inputting everything in, sharing your results, checking your friend's results, etc.

4. *Lack of Control*—a persistent desire or unsuccessful effort to cut down or control use of the tracker and/or exercise/calorie counting

5. *Time*—a great deal of time is spent in activities necessary to obtain the results your tracker tells you that you need to do (e.g., physical activity vacations, spending hours pouring over nutrition labels at the grocery store)

6. *Reductions in Other Activities*—social, occupational, or recreational activities are given up or reduced because of exercise or obsession with calories and calorie tracking

7. *Continuance*—continue to restrict calories or exercise despite knowledge of having a persistent or recurrent physical or psychological problem that is likely to have been caused or exacerbated by the use of the tracker (e.g., continued running despite injury).

If you meet three or more of the above criteria, you may be developing an addiction to your fitness tracker and may end up sick or injured for your efforts. If, on the other hand, none of these were red flags for you, then you are probably fine to continue using your tracker. Just keep an eye out for warning signs that your use of the tracker and/or calorie counting or activity levels are becoming obsessive or unhealthy.

Bottom line: You know your body best as well as your triggers and your limits. Use trackers if you want, but proceed with caution.

11

Activity Trackers Are a Healthy Fitness Monitoring Tool

Tyler Hayes

Tyler Hayes is a freelance writer based in southern California and an early adopter of technology who tries and reports on many new gadgets.

Because people tend to think they exercise more than they actually do and also eat less than they actually do, using an activity tracker can provide a revealing look at day-to-day behaviors that might very well surprise them and help them make positive lifestyle changes—even if they are not especially interested in tracking workouts or counting calories to lose weight. The uniquely individual information and feedback supplied by trackers creates an incentive for the user that is highly personal. An activity tracker isn't for everyone, but even a fit-enough, healthy-enough person can benefit from using one.

The gadget lover in me always swoons over the fitness trackers from the likes of Fitbit, Jawbone, and Basis, among others. The latest models are packed with sensors that can detect UV (ultra violet) light, perspiration, and even sleep states.

But the realist in me soon objects: I've never been overweight, I've never had any health-related issues, and I don't have exercise sessions I need to track. In other words, I'm like a lot of people, somewhere in the vast grey area between fitness fanatic and couch potato. Could I still benefit from wearing a fitness tracker?

I'm a perfect candidate in a lot of other ways, considering I sit and type for a considerable amount of time throughout the day. I should be moving more and find something to help facilitate that. Are there benefits beyond tracking exercise for weight loss, or does a fit-enough, healthy-enough person have nothing to gain from slapping one on?

My existing habits failed miserably at reaching the goal for the first few days.

I decided to indulge my love for the gadgetry and see whether lifestyle benefits would follow. And the results surprised me.

I started innocently enough with a Misfit Flash worn around my wrist. Considering its $50 price tag, waterproof capabilities, and sleep tracking, the Flash was one of the more accessible options to try off the bat. I didn't take it off and I kept it synced to my phone each day.

Since I didn't plan to actually start exercising just so I could use a fitness tracker, I set the bar low with a daily goal of 600 points, which is the equivalent of an hour of walking or about 20 minutes of running. It seemed simple enough, but my existing habits failed miserably at reaching the goal for the first few days.

I thought it was a fluke, but the days kept coming and I still wasn't reaching the goal without actively trying. Apparently I wasn't moving around on my own as much as I had thought. That's one of the first things I discovered after reluctantly participating in the fitness tracking sub-culture.

Perception Is Deception

Apparently walking between the dining room table and the kitchen, or chasing after a two-year-old and a four-year-old isn't as physically strenuous as I had previously imagined. Little bits of movement also take a long time to add up— much longer than I thought, I guess.

At my previous retail job, I could easily spend six of the eight hours on my feet moving around, but now at what equates to an office job, I can't rely on forced movement. This will vary wildly for people, but those sitting at a desk all day can probably relate.

Wearing the activity-tracking device has provided a look into my actual activity—or very close—versus how much I thought I was moving throughout the day. It can be a reality check to see the real numbers or graphs day after day, compared to just trying to think back and remember. The results might surprise you.

I was initially wary about the accuracy of the Misfit Flash's sleep tracking, but after weeks of testing, its results appear at least plausible. Without prompting or fiddling, it has accurately pegged the precise time I fall asleep, so I can only assume it's also doing a fair job at deciphering my deep sleep from my light sleep.

The end game isn't anything magical, just simple ways to affect overall healthiness.

I didn't make any adjusts to my sleeping patterns initially. Looking back, I typically ended up in bed anywhere between 10:30 p.m. and 1 a.m. It only took about a week to see a slight pattern emerge. When I was asleep around 11 p.m., or earlier, I slept better. Not just longer, obviously, but I had more and longer periods of deeper sleep.

It's been interesting to see the correlation between how I feel in the mornings and what the numbers say after syncing the Flash. More often than not, when I feel more rested, I've gotten more than three and a half hours of restful sleep. When I don't, that number has been consistently around two or two and a half hours.

Numbers Aren't Everything

I'm not motivated by calories or steps or distance in the area of health. Maybe I will be in the future as I grow older, but up until now, I have had no interest in these raw metrics.

But the Misfit does a pretty good job of dressing up raw data with a point system and clear graphs. This helps make a simple goal more attainable—in this case that goal is an hour of walking or 20 minutes of running. The end game isn't anything magical, just simple ways to affect overall healthiness.

Microsoft is taking things to a much deeper level by detecting different types of activity and acting as a coach for workout sessions. The company's Band will let you know when it's time to switch to a different activity, among other things.

When the tracking device began to affect positive change, even just slightly, I realized why even someone like me, outside the target market, would still wear one.

Lots of other fitness companies are moving past pumping out raw data and are doing more things beyond just exposing those numbers to the user. Goals, colorful charts and point systems create a wider appeal, and make the trackers that use them a lot more intriguing compared to simple counters.

The Incentive You Didn't Know Existed

I didn't think I needed any incentive to move more. In fact, I was a little spiteful at the insinuation that this tracker could provide that. What's the difference between knowing you walk more and an app telling you the same thing?

I kept the Flash synced for the first week, mostly because it was easy enough. All I had to do with an iPhone 6 was open the Misfit app (available for iOS and Android) and it would sync within 15 or 20 seconds—done. Slowly, syncing wasn't just about getting the data into my phone, but about actually seeing my progress and then thinking about how I could improve that over the rest of the day.

That was the turning point for me. When the tracking device began to affect positive change, even just slightly, I realized why even someone like me, outside the target market, would still wear one.

Fitness Trackers Are More than Hype

I still wouldn't say every single person should be wearing a fitness tracker. But if you have any curiosity or desire to get more active on a day-to-day basis, I would say you're a perfect candidate to give it a shot.

Wearing a tracker is low impact; there's nothing lost other than the money you spent on the device. And that isn't much anymore.

Sleep tracking is still one of the more interesting aspects of these newer and more sophisticated devices. Figuring out ways to improve sleep could be a game changer that may have a real effect on your life and relationships—just as much as staying active throughout the day.

I'm still not overly interested in my health just for the sake of it—the Flash device hasn't changed that—but having a little more insight into my daily activity has given me pause. And who knows, it may end up helping to tack on a few more years.

12

Online Gaming Addiction Can Cause a Host of Mental Health Problems

Han-Ting Wei et al.

The following viewpoint was written by Han-Ting Wei and three other authors—Mu-Hong Chen, Po-Cheng Huang, and Ya-Mei Bai. Han-Ting Wei and Mu-Hong Chen practice in the department of psychiatry at Taipei Veterans General Hospital in Taiwan. Po-Cheng Huang works for the department of rehabilitation at Taipei Hospital in Taiwan, and Ya-Mei Bai is a psychiatrist and faculty member in the psychiatry department at National Yang-Ming University in Taiwan.

In the first study of its kind, researchers in Taiwan investigated the characteristics of online gamers and the relationship between the amount of time spent gaming online and social phobia and depression. The results showed that male online gamers who spent a higher number of hours per week playing had a longer history of gaming and more severe symptoms of anxiety and social phobia, depression, and Internet addiction. Female gamers played fewer hours and had shorter gaming histories but reported more severe somatic, pain, and social phobia symptoms. For both groups, depressive symptoms increased in severity with longer weekly gaming hours.

Online gaming technology has developed rapidly within the past decade, and its related problems have received increasing attention. However, there are few studies on the psychiatric symptoms associated with excessive use of online games. The aim of this study is to investigate the characteristics of online gamers, and the association between online gaming hours, social phobia, and depression using an internet survey.

An online questionnaire was designed and posted on a popular online game website, inviting the online gamers to participate [in] the survey. The content of the questionnaire included demographic data, profiles of internet usage and online gaming, and self-rating scales of Depression and Somatic Symptoms Scale (DSSS), Social Phobia Inventory (SPIN), and Chen Internet Addiction Scale (CIAS). . . .

In recent years, internet addiction has been regarded as an increasingly significant public health issue. A range of studies have demonstrated that a high prevalence of internet addiction in adolescents and young adult population is associated with evident psychiatric problems and serious functional impairment. Greek, Siomos et al.'s study revealed that 8.2% of 2200 adolescent students aged between 12 to 18 had meet the criteria of the Diagnostic Questionnaire for Internet Addiction. In US, Christakis et al. assessed 307 college students at two US universities using the Internet Addiction Test and the Patient Health Questionnaire, noting that 4% of students scored in the problematic or addicted range, and identifying a significant association between problematic internet usage and moderate to severe depression. Among 50 adult patients with internet addiction, Bernadi et al. observed that 14% had a diagnosis of attention deficit and hyperactivity disorder, 15% generalized anxiety disorder, 15% social anxiety disorder, and 7% dysthymia. In Taiwan, Tsai et al. identified 17.9% of university students meet the criteria of internet addiction group using the Chinese Internet Addiction Scale-Revision (CIAS-

R), and the risk factors included male gender, habit of skipping breakfast, mental health morbidity, deficient social support, and neurotic personality traits.

Online Games and Functional Impairment

The technology of online gaming has rapidly developed within the past decade, with online games becoming one of the major daily entertainments for millions of people. Prior research identified that, among the internet activities, online gaming plays an important role on internet addiction, associating with poorer prognosis and more severe social impairments. Griffiths et al. reported that 80% of online gamers sacrificed at least one element of their lives, such as sleep, work, education, and socializing with friends, family, and partners, to play online games. The younger the players, the longer the time they dedicated to playing online games, associating with the further functional impairment. There are four main attractions to online gaming. First, the original game design: the soundtrack, frames, background story, and the complexity of the gaming elements. Second, the role playing achievements: the online gamers may experience new virtual roles, gaining satisfaction from building up characters within levels, accumulating online resources, experiencing online adventures, and receiving online rewards. Third, online social interactions: the gamers may form virtual relationships, gaining online friends, lovers, virtual business, and conducting other types of online activities. Fourth, psychological needs and motivations: online games provide players with outlets for unsatisfying needs and motivations in the real life; within the online game world, players can acquire those they are seeking in the real life, most of the times in an easier way, which motivates them to keep on gaming. The craving for online gaming and substance dependence may share similar neurobiological mechanisms, thus inducing analogous behavioral effects such as excessive usage, severe withdrawal symptoms, tolerance, and negative repercussions. Although there are many previous related studies on internet addiction, few studies specifically focus on the online gaming and associated psychiatric problem. The aim of this study was, therefore, to investigate the characteristics of online gamers and the association between online gaming hours, social phobia, and depression, using an internet survey.

Study Methodology

An online questionnaire was designed and posted from August 1 to August 31, 2010 on the most popular online game websites in Taiwan (PTT BBS and 3 C gamer) to invite the online gamers [to] participate [in] the survey. The participant had to fill out the online informed consent; which explained the answers will be analyzed only for the research purpose, and there is no way to link the data to their true identity. After filling out the online informed consent, the participants would answer an online questionnaire. All participants were assigned a random number in the survey by the server, and they didn't have to fill out the name. Experiments were conducted in accordance with the Declaration of Helsinki and approved by the Institutional Review Board of Taipei Veterans General Hospital. Online agreed informed consent was obtained from all the subjects with adequate understanding of the study.

Higher CIAS scores indicated increased severity of Internet addiction.

The questionnaire [was comprised] of five sections: 1) Demographic information, including age, gender, education years, etc.; 2) Profiles of internet usage and online gaming, including weekday and weekend online gaming hours and total internet hours, history of past online gaming years, etc.; 3) Depression and Somatic Symptoms Scale (DSSS); 4) Social Phobia Inventory (SPIN); 5) Chen's Internet Addiction Scale (CIAS).

Assessment Scales

The Depression and Somatic Symptoms Scale (DSSS) is a 22-item self-administered rating scale, including three subscales as the Depression Subscale (DS), Pain Subscale (PS), and Somatic Subscale (SS). The DS had 12 items, including three vegetative symptoms and fatigue, and the SS had 10 items, including five pain items, which comprised the 5-items pain subscale (PS). Each item is rated with 0–3 score: 0 (not at all); 1 (mild); 2 (moderate); 3 (severe). The range of the sum score is thus 0–66. The scale had good validity and reliability, and higher the scores demonstrate heavier the symptoms.

Social Phobia Inventory (SPIN) is a 17-item self-administered rating scale for evaluating the severity of social phobic symptoms, including three components: Fear in social situations (6 items), avoidance of performance or social situations (7 items), and physiological discomfort in social situations (4 items). Participants were asked to score the distress of each symptoms according to the frequency during the past week: 0 (not at all); 1 (a little bit); 2 (somewhat); 3 (very much); or 4 (extremely). The scale had good validity and reliability, and higher the scores demonstrate heavier the symptoms.

Chen's Internet Addiction Scale (CIAS) is a 26-item self-administered rating scale for internet addiction, including 5 dimensions: Compulsive use, Withdrawal, Tolerance, Problems of interpersonal relationships, and Health and Time management. The total scores of the CIAS ranged from 26 to 104. Higher CIAS scores indicated increased severity of Internet addiction. The scale had good validity and reliability.

Statistical Analysis

Statistical analysis was performed using Statistical Package for Social Science (SPSS) version 17 software (SPSS Inc, Chicago, IL). Analysis of Variance (ANOVA) and Pearson chi-square test were applied to compare the continuous (age, years of

education, years of online gaming, DSSS score, DSSS-DS/
PS/SS subscale scores, CIAS score, SPIN score) and categorical
(gender) variables among the four groups of online gamers
according to weekly online gaming hours. Bonferroni post-
hoc analysis was performed to investigate the significance of
CIAS scores, DSSS scores, DSSS-DS/PS/SS scores, and SPIN
scores among four groups of online gamers. Correlation test
was also performed to investigate the correlation among
weekly online gaming hours, DSSS scores, SPIN scores, and
CIAS scores. Effects of gender on psychiatric symptoms and
patterns of online gaming among the two genders were also
analyzed. The linear regression model was performed to determine the predictors of addictive symptoms (CIAS score) and
depressive symptoms in the online gamers. All statistics were
two-tailed and a p value of <0.05 was considered significant.

---

*Addicted gamers self-reported significantly higher rates
(3 times more) of irritability, daytime sleepiness, sleep
deprivation due to play, low mood and emotional changes
since online gaming onset.*

Survey Results

A total of 722 online gamers, with a mean age of 21.8 ± 4.9
years, completed the online survey within one month. 601
(83.2%) participants were males and 121 (16.8%) were females. Regarding the effects of working days and holidays on
online gaming playing in Wenzel et al.'s study that online
gamers were divided into four groups by daily online game
time (less than 1 hour daily, 1–2 hours daily, 2–4 hours daily,
and > 4 hours daily), the weekly online gaming hours was
deemed as the observed parameter in our study. The mean
weekly online gaming time was 28.2 ± 19.7 hours. The online
gamers were divided into four groups according to their
weekly online gaming time: less than 20 hours (n = 297,

41%), 20 to 40 hours (n = 270, 37%), 40 to 60 hours (n = 112, 16%), and more than 60 hours (n = 43, 6.0%). Among the four groups, male gender, and longer history of online gaming significantly associated with longer weekly online gaming hours. There were no significant differences in age and years of education between the groups. . . .

Our results showed a positive correlation between weekly online gaming hours and internet addiction symptom. The results were consistent with Ko et al.'s study showing a positive correlation between total online gaming hours and total CIAS score, indicating that excessive use of online games resulted in higher risk of internet addiction, leading to more functional impairment, including failure to fulfill obligations at work, school, and home, and decreased participation in social or recreational activities.

Gaming and Depression

Our results also showed a positive correlation between online gaming hours and depressive symptom (DSSS-Depressive Subscale), somatic symptom (DSSS-Somatic Subscale), and Pain symptom (DSSS-Pain Subscale). The association of depressive symptoms was consistent with the findings of Schimit et al.'s study that subjects with online video game dependency spent longer hours per week playing games, had higher scores for loneness or isolation, higher scores for depression, lower scores for social belonging in real life, lower scores for self-esteem, and reduced ability to cope with emotional problems compared with those without dependency. In Achab et al.'s study comparing the characteristics of addict vs non-addict online gamers, these addicted gamers self-reported significantly higher rates (3 times more) of irritability, daytime sleepiness, sleep deprivation due to play, low mood and emotional changes since online gaming onset. Furthermore, self-reported negative consequences of computer game playing increased strongly with average daily playing time and the prevalence of sleeping problems, depression, suicide ideations, anxiety, and obsessions/compulsions increased with increasing playing time in Wenzel et al.'s study. Previously, investigators have proposed that subjects with depression use the internet excessively as a means of self-medicating, and that internet addiction itself could also cause depressive symptoms. Internet addiction and depression may share similar risk factors, such as environment, genes, education, or stress-coping skills, and each might serve to exacerbate the severity of the other. In terms of personality traits, previous studies identified that individuals with online game addiction, especially the Massive Multiplayer Online Role Playing Games (MMORPG), had more aggressive and narcissistic tendencies, less self-control, fewer real world achievements, and lower self-esteem than normal individuals. However, further investigation is needed to elucidate the common mechanisms underlying internet addiction and depression.

[Female gamers] . . . had shorter histories of online gaming and shorter weekly online gaming hours, but had more severe somatic, pain, and social phobic symptoms than the male players.

Online Gaming and Physical Pain

For the association of online gaming hours and somatic/pain symptoms, it might be explained that excessive game-playing lead to muscle soreness, dry eyes, sleep deprivation, inadequate exercising, and even changes in dietary habits. However, previous studies had shown the patients with depression had more somatic and pain symptoms. Half the depressed patients reported multiple unexplained somatic symptoms, and denied psychological symptoms of depression on direct questioning. Some previous studies have suggested that patients in non-Western countries are more likely to report somatic symptoms than are patients in Western countries. The presence of any physical symptom increased the likelihood of a diagnosis of a mood or anxiety disorder by at least twofold to three-fold. These online gamers might not identify their depression, but feel many somatic symptoms such as headache, chest tightness, and muscle pain [that] make them [unable to] focus on school or work, and just spent much time on online game. For the clinical implication, the online gamer who complains [of] many somatic and pain symptoms, we should pay attention to the possibility of depression.

Online Gaming and Social Anxiety

Our results also demonstrated a positive correlation between online gaming hours and social anxiety symptoms by SPIN score. These results suggest that players who suffer from social phobic symptoms are more likely to indulge in the virtual reality provided by online games to avoid real life face to face social distress. Previous studies had shown the individuals with internet addiction had psychopathological characteristics of low self-esteem, low self-perception, and low confidence, but this social detachment in internet could result in further interpersonal frustrations in players' real lives. Achab et al. demonstrated online gamers with positive dependence Adapted Scale had more social, financial, marital, family, and/or professional difficulties since they started online gaming. These findings highlighted the importance of identifying the problem of social anxiety/phobia when treating excessively using online gamers.

Gender Differences

Another interesting finding is the gender difference. In our present study, 121 (16.8%) of the participants were female, with similar ages, years of education, and CIAS scores to the male online gamers. Females form a smaller proportion of the online gaming population. They also had shorter histories of online gaming and shorter weekly online gaming hours, but had more severe somatic, pain, and social phobic symptoms than the male players. The regression model also indicated the female gender is a predictor of depression according to DSSS score. Actually, the gender difference has been identified in previous studies of substance addiction. Tuchman et al. reported gender differences in motivations for substance abuse, with females more likely to use illicit drugs for self-medication of depression or as a means of coping with stressful life events. Women with substance-use problems are with more familial circumstances such as domestic violence, over-responsibility and divorce as high impact factors that lead to drug abuse. Among 425 undergraduate students with problematic internet use, Hetzel-Riggin et al. reported that depression, keeping to oneself, and decreased tension increased problematic internet use in female online gamers. In general, the majority of online gamers were males, these female online gamers had shorter histories of online gaming and shorter weekly online gaming hours, but had more severe somatic, pain, and social phobic symptoms than the male players. The results indicated these female players tend to engage in online games as a means of coping with depression, somatic symptoms, pain symptoms, and social anxiety. From the clinical point of view, the female online gamer might be with higher risk of depression.

Limitations of the Study

To our best knowledge, this is the first study to investigate excessive online game hours and its association with depressive, social phobic, and internet addiction symptoms. However, there were some limitations. First, the enlisting of study subjects via invitation from online gaming websites introduces selection bias, thus the validity of their responses cannot be ensured. Second, the study is a descriptive, cross-sectional study. A prospective study would have represented a more meaningful means of evaluating the causal relationship between long hours spent playing online games and depression, social phobia, and internet addiction. Third, diagnoses of internet addiction, depression and social phobia could not be confirmed through self-completed questionnaires. Further investigation by face-to-face interview is needed to validate the findings. Fourth, the positive correlation between time spent on gaming and the internet addiction scale may be different for the subgroup of people with highly skilled hobbies or professions. In our survey, we didn't identify this factor, and it deserves further research.

In conclusion, in the study population, online gamers who played excessively had higher incidence of comorbidities including internet addiction, depression, and social phobia. Depressive symptoms increased in severity with longer weekly online gaming hours, female gender, and severity of social phobia symptoms. These findings could prove useful when devising future strategies for prevention and intervention of problematic online gaming habits.

13

Online Gaming Can Help Ease Social Anxiety

Anastasia Wythe

Anastasia Wythe is a transgender writer, games critic, and gamer who writes for Gamemoir's LGBT & Gender section, and has also contributed to FemHype and theFLOUNCE. Wythe has a lifetime of experience playing video games and has also contributed to Huffington Post Live *and the* BBC World Service *as a guest on trigger warning discussions.*

Online gaming is frequently a solitary hobby and many people who are drawn to it are introverts who have a hard time interacting socially with others. Those who have social anxiety disorder (SAD), like this viewpoint's author, may find that gaming online allows them to gingerly explore ways of connecting with others in a way that feels safe to them. The games themselves can also help foster a shared social experience and create a sense of belonging for such individuals. Connecting and socializing with other gamers online, even a little bit, can help people with anxiety overcome some of the issues they struggle with every day.

Most of my close friends don't realize it, but I'm more of an introvert than anything else. Very often, that means playing video games by myself at home. Suffice to say, gaming is one of my favorite hobbies, and has been a core interest of mine throughout my entire life.

Introversion isn't exactly uncommon in video gaming, either. Like reading and writing, hardcore gaming is often a solitary hobby—done alone, often for an extended period of time. And, despite the ever-growing presence of massively multiplayer gaming, it's quite common to have very few online friends. Many gamers exclusively play single-player games, which lack any meaningful online connectivity. Other times, multiplayer video games allow us to play online without needing to communicate with others. *Team Fortress 2* and *Battlefield 4*, for instance, utilize strategic team-based gameplay that still gives lone wolves the opportunity to play without needing a friend to tag along. Of course, with little need to build friendships in-game . . . being a gamer can get lonely at times.

Introversion is relatively common among gamers. . . . Because video games are so engaging, gaming often attracts us introverts.

Growing up, this was a bit of a problem for me, as I often felt isolated from others—both offline and online. I had very few strong, meaningful friendships, and relied on video games as a form of self-medication. I began going through therapy for growing issues with depression and anxiety that I experienced on a regular basis.

It wasn't until high school that I was diagnosed with general anxiety disorder. I also found out that I had social anxiety disorder—a debilitating mental illness based around strong fears of judgement, personal interaction, and social approval from others. Social anxiety disorder led me to isolate myself from others, often spending my free time playing video games and browsing the Internet.

A Burgeoning Identity Crisis

Apparently, I'm not alone either. According to the Anxiety and Depression Association of America, social anxiety disorder regularly affects 15 million Americans. And, while not every gamer might have diagnosed social anxiety, many can relate to recurring shyness in offline life.

Introversion is relatively common among gamers. Gaming allows us to explore hundreds of worlds without leaving the house, and hardcore video games often require an enormous time investment towards a specific goal—such as learning how to play a complex strategy game, or perfecting resource management. Because video games are so engaging, gaming often attracts us introverts.

Introversion is something to be cherished, not rejected. However, gaming has been deeply under-appreciated over the past few decades, and mainstream media coverage on gaming has rarely helped us come out of our shells.

Since the early 90s, moral panic has consistently surrounded video gaming. Parents, pundits, and politicians continue to complain that video games lead to delinquency, violent crimes, and (gasp!) introversion among teens. And, as gaming struggles to be taken seriously within both mainstream and alternative pop culture, many gamers feel extremely isolated from others. It's hard to fawn over video games' artistic merits when your friends don't even understand what a "Mass Effect" is.

In other words, being a gamer is incredibly confusing, and we're often told that our hobbies are juvenile—regardless of how meaningful, and powerful, video games are to us. And, when our friends aren't gamers ... well, it's hard to explain why video games are so influential in our lives.

"Even on a Battlefield?"

Due to my history of social anxiety, obsessive-compulsive disorder, and self-medication via video games, I'm ... well, a gamer with an immense amount of baggage about my hobby. In real life, I often feel like I have very few outlets to discuss gaming. And many gamers seem to feel the same way.

However, we often forget something—gaming comes with very real and meaningful personal experiences. When we play video games, we are not just playing by ourselves; we're engaging in a community and culture with similarly shared experiences. And these connections can help us build close friendships, and connect with others.

The games that we play help us connect with one another, and build meaningful personal connections.

Gamers are literally a market identity. When we purchase video games, we buy into the market. We vote with our wallets, and tell the industry, "Hey, this is a game I like." And thousands upon thousands of fans partake in this odd economic ritual *per day*. We buy games and play them—and we end up sharing the same characters, narratives, universes, and gameplay experiences across the gaming community.

We build memories around video games, and they become meaningful experiences. For instance—do you remember when Commander Shepard had to sacrifice a crew member on Virmire in *Mass Effect 1*? How about when Solid Snake laid Sniper Wolf to rest in *Metal Gear Solid*? Do you remember Otacon asking Snake, "Do you think love can bloom, even on a battlefield?" Many gamers can remember these moments verbatim, down to the tone and inflection of Snake's voice. Why? Because we each experience deep and personal moments within these interactive narratives. As a result, we often share these experiences together as gamers.

Games Help Players Connect

Granted, it's easy to feel that we're isolated from each other. Sometimes, it feels like gamers are few and far between in real life. However, the games that we play help us connect with one another, and build meaningful personal connections.

These shared moments bring gamers together, and build a sense of community around video gaming.

Other solutions exist as well, to help gamers with social anxiety and introversion. For many socially anxious individuals, we fear being judged. Judgment becomes an extremely uncomfortable experience, to the point where we might avoid communicating with others.

However, video games can help us overcome this fear, because of gaming's minimal in-game communication features. During a casual match of *Killing Floor*, for instance, players can talk to others via voice chat. While this might seem extremely frightening at first, non-competitive multiplayer video games often allow gamers to drop in and out of using a mic with relative ease. And games with friendly communities and strong server moderation teams often help moderate voice chat, and kick out harassers and trolls. In other words, a gamer who wants to talk over mic can give voice chat a shot—and, if they feel comfortable, they can gradually slip into using a mic. Or, if they feel uncomfortable, they can simply back out. Either way, online chat services allow players to practice speaking up, and pull out if they feel uncomfortable.

Control of Social Interactions

As I've continued to struggle with using my voice in-game, I've found this kind of laxity extremely helpful. When I began hosting let's plays and twitch streams on my YouTube channel last year, I was extremely nervous about my voice—due to a mixture of both gender dysphoria and social anxiety. However, knowing that I was able to start and stop recordings at will gradually soothed my nerves, and helped ease me into hosting hour-long streams. Not to mention, receiving positive support from my Twitter followers encouraged me to become more extroverted, and break out of my gaming shell.

Granted, social anxiety is not a disorder that can be overcome with twitch streams and video games. Social anxiety disorder is a very real and debilitating illness, which requires proper mental health care and cognitive therapy. However, little steps along the way can be massively beneficial for socially anxious gamers. Connecting and socializing with other gamers can help us overcome some of the issues we regularly face, and help us fight these struggles as we play.

The Constant Lure of Smartphones Is Bad for Children's Mental Health

Peter Stanford

Peter Stanford is a staff writer for the Telegraph *newspaper in the United Kingdom.*

Child psychotherapists are noticing a spike in the number of serious mental health problems among children, and some attribute the difficulties to their growing use of Internet-connected technologies, such as smartphones. The amount of time that children spend online is one factor that can impact mental health, but another is the type of content that children are able to access on smartphones because there is little parental supervision of their use. Websites that feature pornography are just one of the obvious concerns; others include sites that provide information about anorexia and other eating disorders, self-harming, and chat rooms where bullying occurs. Parents should monitor their children's technology consumption and set a good example with their own smartphone use.

Julie Lynn Evans has been a child psychotherapist for 25 years, working in hospitals, schools and with families, and she says she has never been so busy.

"In the 1990s, I would have had one or two attempted suicides a year—mainly teenaged girls taking overdoses, the things that don't get reported. Now, I could have as many as four a month."

And it's not, she notes, simply a question of her reputation as both a practitioner and a writer drawing so many people to the door of her cosy consulting rooms in west London where we meet. "If I try to refer people on, everyone else is choc-a-bloc too. We are all saying the same thing. There has been an explosion in numbers in mental health problems amongst youngsters."

[UK] Care Minister, Norman Lamb, has this week been promising a "complete overhaul" of the system that deals with these troubled tweens and teens, after a Department of Health report highlighted the negative impact of funding cuts. And the three main party leaders have all made encouraging pre-election noises about putting more resources into mental health services.

I am seeing the evidence in the numbers of depressive, anorexic, cutting children who come to see me. And it always has something to do with the computer, the Internet and the smartphone.

Yet, while the down-to-earth Lynn Evans welcomes the prospect of additional funding, this divorced, Canadian-born mother of three grown up children, isn't convinced that it is the solution to the current crisis.

The floodgates of desperate youngsters opened, she recalls, in 2010. "I saw my work increase by a mad amount and so did others I work with. Suddenly everything got much more dangerous, much more immediate, much more painful."

Official figures confirm the picture she paints, with emergency admissions to child psychiatric wards doubling in four years, and those young adults hospitalised for self-harm up by 70 per cent in a decade.

"Something is clearly happening," she says, "because I am seeing the evidence in the numbers of depressive, anorexic, cutting children who come to see me. And it always has something to do with the computer, the Internet and the smartphone."

"Pocket Rockets"

Issues such as cyber-bullying are, of course, nothing new, and schools now all strive to develop robust policies to tackle them, but Lynn Evans' target is both more precise and more general. She is pointing a finger of accusation at the smartphones—"pocket rockets" as she calls them—which are now routinely in the hands of over 80 per cent of secondary school age children. Their arrival has been, she notes, a key change since 2010.

"It's a simplistic view, but I think it is the ubiquity of broadband and smartphones that has changed the pace and the power and the drama of mental illness in young people."

With a smartphone—as opposed to an earlier generation of "brick" mobiles that could only be used to keep in touch with worried parents—youngsters can now, she says, "access the internet without adult supervision in parks, on street, wherever they are, and then they can go anywhere. So there are difficult chat rooms, self-harming websites, anorexia websites, pornography, and a whole invisible world of dark places. In real life, we travel with our children. When they are connected via their smartphone to the web, they usually travel alone."

She quotes one website that has come up in conversations with youngsters in the consulting room. "I wouldn't have known about it otherwise, but it is where men masturbate in real time while children as young as 12 watch them. So parents think their children are upstairs in their bedrooms with their friends having popcorn and no alcohol, yet this is the sort of thing they are watching. And as they watch, they are saying, 'this is what sex is.' It is leaving them really distressed."

Parents Must Do More

Mums and dads who allow young teenagers to have smartphones—and she wouldn't say yes until they were 14—must also take a more active role in policing the use of them, she says, however unpopular it will make them with their offspring.

Harmful, too, is the sheer length of exposure to the virtual world via their smartphones that youngsters have now.

"I think children should have privacy within their own rooms and in their diaries, and I think they should have the Internet, but I don't think they should have both, certainly not until they have proved they are completely safe and reliable. So, check their browser history, look at their Facebook, Instagram, and then discuss it with them.

"When they are 15, you don't, for example, let them go to pubs, or stay out in the local park at four in morning, yet they'll get into much less trouble physically there than they will on their smartphones on the internet. I'm not talking about paedophiles preying on them. I'm talking about anorexia sites and sites where they will be bullied."

That is where the damage is being done to their mental health, she argues. Harmful, too, is the sheer length of exposure to the virtual world via their smartphones that youngsters have now. Her strong advice to parents is to limit access. "Use it like parents used to use TV with their children. 'You can watch this but you can't watch that,' and there's a watershed. We need that kind of discipline."

No Internet Is as Bad as Too Much

How about just banning it altogether? "I believe that parents who don't allow the Internet can cause as much damage as parents who allow too much. Their children are not able to work and play and be with the rest of the children in the playground. It has to be about balance, not banning."

Living so much in a virtual world has other negative consequences, she suggests. It gives young users no time to reflect or learn about the consequences of their actions. "So if you are having a WhatsApp chat with your friends, and it all goes very wrong, you can say to them, 'I wish you were dead.' Now perfectly nice children find themselves saying, 'I wish you were dead,' because they haven't got time to reflect, and then their words go everywhere. Kindness, compassion, ethics, it's all out of the window when you are in this instantaneous gossip world with no time to think, and no time to learn about having relationships."

[Children] need to find a sense of purpose by connecting with other people, not being on the Internet all the time.

Attachment Issues

Parents also need to think about what example they set their children by their own attachment to their smartphones. "We know all about the importance of childhood attachment and good healthy childhood relationships with parents. Yet, if you look in the local park, you see children at a very early age not getting the tender, intense love they used to because their parents are always on their smartphones. Put them down, and be with your kids from day one. They're not getting what they need from us to build up their core sense of self and that can create the problems I see down the line."

Julie Lynn Evans is, in one way, a reluctant campaigner. She is keen to point out that this isn't happening to all children, and that there are other potential causes for the current crisis—"results-driven school programmes," busy parents and the recession are three she quotes, not to mention "organic" mental health such as schizophrenia.

And, she says, she has enough on her plate, dealing daily with the current crisis in adolescent mental health, without getting drawn into a broader argument about how to tackle its root causes. Indeed, she confesses that two weeks ago she was so exhausted that she even contemplated giving up work altogether.

"I was dealing with a young boy who had just jumped out of a car and run into oncoming traffic. Two psychiatrists and I were tearing our hair out trying to find a safe place to put him. We tried for four hours to find him a hospital bed, and there was nowhere for him, no hospital bed available. He ended up going home and we put in nurses 24 hours a day, but not a lot of people are going to be able to do that. At the end of it, I was so tired I thought I can't go on."

A "Broken" System

What makes her continue, though, in a system that even Norman Lamb has called "broken," is that what she is witnessing frightens her. And she is speaking out because she believes the problem can be fixed.

She is emphatically not anti-Internet, but rather anti-the negative side effects of it on our young. "It is battering our children's brains. They have no times for the goodies in life— kindness, acceptance, conversation, face-to-face, nature, nurture. They need to find a sense of purpose by connecting with other people, not being on the Internet all the time."

If parents and schools engage with it openly and together, this can be tackled, she urges. "If we can grab what's going on by the horns, and do something about it, then I am optimistic. I'm not optimistic, though, if we just say it's the government's fault and we've got to have more money."

Organizations to Contact

The editors have compiled the following list of organizations concerned with the issues debated in this book. The descriptions are derived from materials provided by the organizations. All have publications or information available for interested readers. The list was compiled on the date of publication of the present volume; the information provided here may change. Be aware that many organizations take several weeks or longer to respond to inquiries, so allow as much time as possible.

American Psychiatric Association
1000 Wilson Blvd., Suite 1825, Arlington, VA   22209-3901
(703) 907-7300
e-mail: apa@psych.org
website: www.psych.org

The American Psychiatric Association is the world's largest psychiatric organization and the primary professional organization for psychiatrists in the United States. The association is best known for publishing the *Diagnostic and Statistical Manual of Mental Disorders (DSM-5)*, the book used worldwide to diagnose psychiatric disorders. The group's website features a collection of position statements, fact sheets, and reports related to a variety of mental health subjects. Among those that concern the Internet and technology use, the article "Smartphone Overuse Growing and Harmful to Adolescents" and a downloadable PDF of the *DSM-5*'s criteria for Internet-Gaming-Disorder maybe of particular interest.

American Psychological Association
750 First St. NE, Washington, DC   20002-4242
(202) 336-5500
website: www.apa.org

The American Psychological Association is the world's largest professional association of psychologists. The organization's website includes dozens of publications related to the Internet and anxiety, including the articles "Facebook: Friend or Foe?," "Social Networking's Good and Bad Impacts on Kids," and "Self-Help Sites: A Blessing or a Bane?"

Anxiety and Depression Association of America (ADAA)

8701 Georgia Ave., Suite 412, Silver Spring, MD   20910
(240) 485-1001
website: www.adaa.org

The Anxiety and Depression Association of America (ADAA) is a national nonprofit organization dedicated to the prevention, treatment, and cure of anxiety and mood disorders, obsessive-compulsive disorder, and post-traumatic stress disorder. The ADAA's mission is to improve the lives of children and adults who suffer from these disorders through education, practice, and research. The ADAA strives to improve patient care by promoting empirically supported treatments and best practices across disciplines. The organization's website features extensive information and resources on anxiety disorders, organized by anxiety type.

Berkman Center for Internet and Society

Harvard University, 23 Everett St., 2nd Floor
Cambridge, MA   02138
(617) 495-7547 • fax: (617) 495-7641
e-mail: cyber@law.harvard.edu
website: http://cyber.law.harvard.edu

The Berkman Center for Internet and Society was founded to explore cyberspace, share in its study, and help pioneer its development. The Center represents a network of faculty, students, fellows, entrepreneurs, lawyers, and virtual architects working to identify and engage with the challenges and opportunities of the digital age. The Center's "Digital Natives" project focuses on the key legal, social, and political implications of a generation "born digital"—those who grow up immersed in digital technologies and for whom a life fully integrated with digital devices is the norm. By understanding young people's interactions with digital media such as Internet, smartphones, and video games, the Center hopes to address the issues their practices raise, learn how to harness the opportunities their digital fluency presents, and shape regulatory and educational frameworks in a way that advances the public interest.

Center for Internet Addiction
website: http://netaddiction.com

Founded in 1995, the Center for Internet Addiction was the first evidenced-based "Digital Detox"™ recovery program to provide treatment for Internet addiction using a specialized form of cognitive-behavioral therapy. The organization's website features a wide array of articles, FAQs, and resources concerning Internet overuse and addiction. Free self-tests available on the site include the Internet Addiction Test (IAT), the first and only psychometric test for Internet addiction, as well as other tests to assess online gaming, gambling, auctioning, and pornography consumption. The site also features resources for family members of those who may have problems with Internet overuse.

Cyberbullying Research Center
website: www.cyberbullying.us

Established in 2005, the Cyberbullying Research Center serves as a clearinghouse of information concerning the ways adolescents use and misuse technology. The organization's website provides research findings, stories, cases, fact sheets, tips and strategies, current headlines, quizzes, a frequently updated blog, and a number of other helpful resources concerning cyberbullying. It also has downloadable materials for educators, counselors, parents, law enforcement officers, and other youth-serving professionals to use and distribute as needed.

Online Gamers Anonymous (OLGA/OLG-Anon)
PO Box 67, Osceola, WI   54020
(612) 245-1115
website: www.olganon.org

Founded in 2002, Online Gamers Anonymous (OLGA/OLG-Anon) is a self-help fellowship that provides a twelve-step program of recovery for excessive game playing, whether it be computer, video, console, or online. The group's online community includes recovering gamers, family members, loved ones, friends, concerned individuals, and those who educate and reach out to others. OLGA/OLG-Anon understands how destructive excessive game playing can be to the real-world lives of gamers and to those close to them, so the group provides resources for open discussion, support, education, and referrals. The OLGA/OLG-Anon community is open to all who seek support, and its message forums are available to all, regardless of bias or opinion.

Pew Internet and American Life Project

1615 L St. NW, Suite 700, Washington, DC   20036
(202) 419-4300 • fax: (202) 419-4349
website: www.pewinternet.org

The Pew Internet and American Life Project is one of seven projects that make up the Pew Research Center, a nonpartisan, nonprofit "fact tank" that provides information on the issues, attitudes, and trends that shape America and the world. The Project produces reports exploring the impact of the Internet on families, communities, work and home, daily life, education, health care, and civic and political life. The Project's website features a wide variety of articles, datasets, presentations, and other resources, including the reports "US Smartphone Use in 2015" and "Teens, Social Media and Technology Overview 2015."

Bibliography

Books

Elias Aboujaoude *Virtually You: The Dangerous Powers of the E-Personality.* New York: W.W. Norton, 2011.

Ann Blair *Too Much to Know: Managing Scholarly Information Before the Modern Age.* New Haven, CT: Yale University Press, 2010.

Joanne Canter *Conquering Cyber Overload.* Madison, WI: CyberOutlook Press, 2010.

Sameer Hinduja and Justin Patchin *Bullying Beyond the Schoolyard: Preventing and Responding to Cyberbullying,* 2nd ed. Thousand Oaks, CA: Sage Publications, 2015.

Julie A. Jacko, ed. *Human-Computer Interaction: New Trends.* New York: Springer, 2009.

William Powers *Hamlet's Blackberry—A Practical Philosophy for Building a Good Life in the Digital Age.* New York: Harper Collins, 2010.

Matt Richtel *A Deadly Wandering: A Tale of Tragedy and Redemption in the Age of Attention.* New York: William Morrow, 2014.

Larry Rosen *iDisorder: Understanding Our Obsession with Technology and Overcoming Its Hold on Us.* New York: Palgrave Macmillan, 2011.

Sherry Turkle   *Alone Together: Why We Expect More from Technology and Less from Each Other.* New York: Basic Books, 2012.

Periodicals and Internet Sources

Elias Aboujaoude   "Cyberbullying: From the Playground to 'Insta,'" *Psychology Today*, January 11, 2015.

Alex Alben   "Op-Ed: I Lost My Smartphone and Lived to Tell About It," *Seattle Times*, March 22, 2013.

Hephzibah Anderson   "Never Heard of Fomo? You're So Missing Out," *Guardian*, April 16, 2011.

Andrea Bartz and Brenna Ehrlich   "Be Careful When Diagnosing Your Ailments Online," CNN, March 12, 2015. www.cnn.com.

Martha Bebinger   "Social Media Anxiety Disorder (SMAD): The Next New Medical Condition?," *Common Health*, April 10, 2012. http://commonhealth.wbur.org.

Mark Becker et al.   "Media Multitasking Is Associated with Symptoms of Depression and Social Anxiety," *Journal of Cyberpsychology, Behavior and Social Networking*, February 2013.

Elizabeth Bernstein	"Thank You for Not Sharing: What Triggers People to Reveal Too Much; Avoiding the Post-Conversation Cringe," *Wall Street Journal*, May 6, 2013.
Nick Bilton	"The Health Concerns in Wearable Tech," *New York Times*, March 18, 2015.
Stephanie Buck	"What Doctors Think About Your Online Health Searches," *Mashable*, June 15, 2012. http://mashable.com.
Melissa Carroll	"UH Study Links Facebook Use to Depressive Symptoms," University of Houston, April 6, 2015. www.uh.edu.
Ariana Eunjung Cha	"The Human Upgrade: The Revolution Will Be Digitized," *Washington Post*, May 9, 2015.
CNN/Money	"Facebook Now Lets You Post When You're Dead," CNN/Money, February 12, 2015. http://money.cnn.com.
Claire Cohen	"FoMo: Do You Have a Fear of Missing Out?," *Telegraph* (UK), May 16, 2013.
Arlin Cuncic	"What Is Cyber Bullying? Learn How to Help Your Socially Anxious Child Cope," about.com, September 30, 2013. http://socialanxietydisorder .about.com.
Carolyn Davis	"The Anxiety of the Absent Phone," *Philadelphia Inquirer*, October 4, 2012.

Arden Dingle and   "Psychiatric Impacts of Video Games,
Jay Kothari   Internet Addiction on Children,"
                      Psychiatry Advisor, February 6, 2015.
                      www.psychiatryadvisor.com.

Economist   "Too Much Information: How to
                      Cope with Data Overload," June 30,
                      2011.

Christina Farr   "Weighing Privacy vs. Rewards of
                      Letting Insurers Track Your Fitness,"
                      National Public Radio, April 9, 2015.
                      www.npr.org.

Britney Fitzgerald "Americans Addicted to Checking
                      Smartphones, Would 'Panic' If They
                      Lost Device (STUDY)," Huffington
                      Post, June 21, 2012.
                      www.huffingtonpost.com.

Britney Fitzgerald "Social Media Is Causing Anxiety,
                      Study Finds," Huffington Post, July 11,
                      2012. www.huffingtonpost.com.

Jeff Foss   "The Tale of a Fitness-Tracking
                      Addict's Struggles with Strava,"
                      Wired, October 3, 2014.

Ellen Gibson   "Psychologists Concerned About
                      Smartphone 'Obsession,'" Huffington
                      Post, July 26, 2011.
                      www.huffingtonpost.com.

Stephanie   "Cyberchondria Could Save Your
Goldberg   Life," CNN, December 6, 2011.
                      www.cnn.com.

Serena Gordon — "Video Game 'Addiction' Tied to Depression, Anxiety in Kids," *HealthDay*, January 17, 2011. http://health.usnews.com.

John Grohol — "FOMO Addiction: The Fear of Missing Out," Psych Central, April 14, 2011. http://psychcentral.com.

Rebecca Harris — "The Loneliness Epidemic: We're More Connected than Ever—But Are We Feeling More Alone?," *Independent* (UK), March 30, 2015.

Pamela Hartzband and Jerome Groopman — "Untangling the Web—Patients, Doctors, and the Internet," *New England Journal of Medicine*, March 25, 2010.

Katia Hetter — "10 Fun Ways to Celebrate Screen-Free Week," CNN, May 4, 2015. www.cnn.com.

Sameer Hinduja and Justin Patchin — "Cyberbullying Fact Sheet: Identification, Prevention, and Response," Cyberbullying Research Center, 2014. www.cyberbullying.us.

Tom Horvath et al. — "Other Activity (or Behavioural) Addictions: Internet Gaming Disorder (Addiction)," AMHC, 2015. www.amhc.org.

Reese Jones — "Five Benefits of Giving Your Kids a Smartphone," EduPad, November 12, 2013. www.edupad.com.

Benjamin Keller "Self-Tracking, to the Point of Obsession," *In Vivo*, November 12, 2014. www.invivomagazine.com.

Jared Keller "We Are All Internet Addicts Now—Just Don't Call It That," *Pacific Standard*, May 30, 2013.

Sarah Knapton "Google 'Makes People Think They Are Smarter than They Are,'" *Telegraph* (UK), March 31, 2015.

Maria Konnikova "Is Internet Addiction a Real Thing?," *New Yorker*, November 26, 2014.

Vicky Kung "Rise of 'Nomophobia': More People Fear Loss of Mobile Contact," CNN, March 7, 2012. www.cnn.com.

Lookout "Mobile Mindset Study," 2012. www.lookout.com.

David Lumb "How Virtual Reality Can Curb Your Social Anxiety," *Fast Company*, June 28, 2013.

Anna Medaris Miller "The Dark Side of Activity Trackers," *U.S. News & World Report*, January 6, 2015.

Lulu Miller and Alix Spiegel "Can a Computer Change the Essence of Who You Are?," National Public Radio, February 13, 2015. www.npr.org.

K. Muse et al. "Cyberchondriasis: Fact or Fiction? A Preliminary Examination of the Relationship Between Health Anxiety and Searching for Health Information on the Internet," *Journal of Anxiety Disorders*, vol. 26, no. 1, 2012.

Catharine Paddock "Facebook Use Feeds Anxiety and Inadequacy Says Small Study," Medical News Today, July 10, 2012. www.medicalnewstoday.com.

Tom Phillips "Chinese Man Who Collapsed After 14-Day Web Binge Begs Paramedics to Turn on His Computer," *Telegraph* (UK), May 4, 2015.

Tom Phillips "Chinese Teen Chops Hand off to 'Cure' Internet Addiction," *Telegraph* (UK), February 3, 2015.

Nathan Sharer "Examining Social Anxiety and Depression Among Excessive Online Gamers," Marshall University, January 1, 2012. http://mds.marshall.edu.

Alexandra Shulman "And Finally . . . Are You Suffering from Compulsive Activity Disorder?," *Daily Mail*, August 5, 2009.

Victor Skinner "Some Students Spending 75% of School Day on iPads," EAG News, June 18, 2015. www.eagnews.org.

Sara Smyth — "Toll of Social Media on Girls' Mental Health: Sexualised Images Fuelling Rise in Anxiety Among Pupils Aged 11 to 13," *Daily Mail*, April 19, 2015.

Julie Spira — "Do You Suffer from Social Media Anxiety Disorder?," *Huffington Post*, January 11, 2013. www.huffingtonpost.com.

Madeline Stone — "Smartphone Addiction Now Has a Clinical Name," *Business Insider*, July 31, 2014.

Jon Swartz — "Social Media Users Grapple with Information Overload," *USA Today*, February 2, 2011.

Josh Tapper — "Internet Addicts Face Constant Temptation, Non-Believers," *Toronto Star*, February 1, 2013.

Aviv Weinstein et al. — "Internet Addiction Is Associated with Social Anxiety in Young Adults," *Annals of Clinical Psychiatry*, February 2, 2015.

Justin White — "Research Finds Link Between Social Media and the 'Fear of Missing Out,'" *Washington Post*, July 8, 2013.

Ryen White and Eric Horvitz — "Experiences with Web Search on Medical Concerns and Self Diagnosis," *AMIA Annual Symposium Proceedings*, November 14, 2009.

David Wong	"6 New Kinds of Anxiety the Internet Gave Us," *Cracked*, April 23, 2013. www.cracked.com.
Jenna Wortham	"Feel Like a Wallflower? Maybe It's Your Facebook Wall," *New York Times*, April 9, 2011.
Ju-Yu Yen et al.	"Social Anxiety in Online and Real-Life Interaction and Their Associated Factors," *Journal of Cyberpsychology, Behavior and Social Networking*, January 2015.

Index